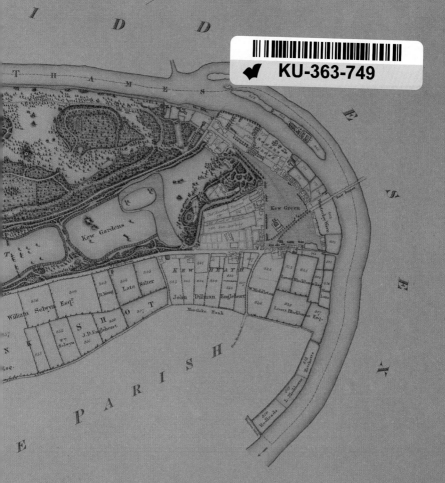

PLAN

of the Royal Manor of

RICHMOND,

otherwise

WEST SHEEN,

in the County of Surry;

in *GRANT* to

HER MAJESTY.

Taken under the Direction of

PETER BURRELL ESQ:

His Majesty's Survr Genl

in 1771, by Thos Richardson in

York Street, Cavendish Square.

The Botanical Adventures of JOSEPH BANKS

Christina Harrison

Kew Publishing
Royal Botanic Gardens, Kew

Contents

This portrait of a handsome young Banks by Sir Joshua Reynolds was completed after Banks's adventures in the South Pacific and Iceland. The globe refers to his extensive travels and the Latin inscription on the papers is said to translate as: 'tomorrow we will sail the vast ocean again'.

© Agnew's, London / Bridgeman Images

Foreword

Through the lens of a citizen of the 21st century, it is hard to comprehend the full extent of the influence of Sir Joseph Banks on the developing British Empire of the late 18th and early 19th centuries. There were few, if any, of his contemporaries who so effectively planned and choreographed the expansion of knowledge and understanding of the natural sciences of that period, laying the foundations for the expansion of the British Empire, and deriving wealth from its newly-discovered, scientifically-based economies. In an age of geographical exploration and discovery, he played a leading role both as a participant, but perhaps more significantly, as a dedicated sponsor, mentor and advocate.

From his early years Banks developed a thirst for knowledge about the natural world, and of plants in particular. The steps he took to ensure that he received, from outside sources, the necessary education in botanical science while studying at the University of Oxford (with agreement of the Chair of Botany) give us an indication of his determination and personal ambition.

As a leading participant and generous sponsor of the *Endeavour* voyage (1768-71), led by Lieutenant James Cook, he visited the exotic South Pacific, ostensibly to observe the transit of Venus, but also to accompany Cook on the perhaps more ambitious mission to discover 'Terra Incognita' – the great unknown southern land, now known as Australia. The discoveries made on this three-year adventure opened the eyes of the world to the diverse and extraordinary flora and fauna of the southern hemisphere and made tangible steps towards completing the jigsaw puzzle of the globe.

When back in England, from 1771, Banks achieved a popularity and realm of influence for which it is difficult to find a modern parallel. His many and varied appointments and achievements are listed in this book and give the reader a vivid picture of the many ways in which he guided and supported, lobbied and at times personally steered the establishment of societies and institutions, not the least being his role as an advisor to King George III on development of the Royal Botanic Gardens at Kew. He was appointed as President of the Royal Society at the relatively young age of 35 (a position he famously held for 41 years) and was a founding member of a number of other key institutions and societies including

Among the many new plant species introduced by Banks and his plant hunters to Britain was *Albuca setosa* from the Cape of Good Hope. Introduced to Kew by collector Francis Masson in 1795. This beautiful illustration was produced for *Curtis's Botanical Magazine*.

the Society for the Improvement of Horticulture (now known as the Royal Horticultural Society) and the Linnean Society.

His influence was not only contained within England, for example, he was the key advocate for the establishment of a colony on the coast of New South Wales in Australia, and was an honorary member of over fifty foreign societies. He personally sponsored, instructed and commissioned various plant collectors to explore far-flung and botanically rich continents in search of new introductions to horticulture and agriculture. Many plants that we now recognise as almost ubiquitous garden staples first arrived in cultivation through Banks's sponsored collection programmes. The collectors themselves were intrepid, resourceful and totally dedicated to their cause. Most died in pursuit of the mission.

In our current parlance, Sir Joseph Banks was one of the most significant influencers of his time. We continue to harvest the benefits of his legacy in so many ways that it is hard to appreciate them fully. This book gives us the rich and intriguing story of his life and reminds us of his lasting impact.

Richard Barley

Director of Horticulture,
Learning & Operations
Royal Botanic Gardens, Kew

Introduction

The life of the great naturalist Sir Joseph Banks is a tale packed with wonderful discoveries, intriguing people, exotic landscapes and botanical adventures. Inside these pages you'll find a celebration of this one man's obsession with plants, and some of his many fascinating achievements. Through the use of objects, letters, books, illustrations and plants from the vast collections of the Royal Botanic Gardens, Kew – an institution that he helped to found – you'll find the story of his life and his self-appointed mission to improve the world through plants.

Banks may be well known to some of you who are familiar with the history of Kew or the natural sciences, but for the majority of people he is an unknown and under-appreciated historical figure. Banks was not your average wealthy Georgian gentleman. Throughout his life he chose to use and increase his influence to gather plants from around the world to – as he saw it – expand the knowledge, wealth and influence of his beloved Britain. From a young age he was full of passion for the natural world and organised his own botanical education. Over his life he collected a vast number of plants new to science, amassed a unique library and created an

SIR JOSEPH BANKS, BARᵗ K.B: P.R.S

OB. 1820.

FROM THE ORIGINAL OF SIR THOMAS LAWRENCE.

THE BRITISH MUSEUM.

Although the epitome of a Georgian gentleman in many ways, Banks was unusual in his passion for natural history and his pursuit of botany for the benefit of the country rather than his own pocket.
Wellcome Collection

Banks collected and 'discovered' many hundreds of plants including the Australian genus that would later be named after him – *Banksia*. This painting by Stella Ross-Craig was completed for *Curtis's Botanical Magazine*, published by Kew in 1942.

influential circle of expert friends. Without his love of plants, he may just have become another member of the wealthy landed gentry rather than one of the most influential men of the Georgian age.

A founding father of Kew, one of the founders of the Royal Horticultural Society, president of the Royal Society and linked to myriad other organisations such as the British Museum and the Linnean Society, Banks's influence spread far and wide. He enjoyed taking part in expeditions to Newfoundland, South America, the Pacific, Australia and even Iceland. He influenced the growing of tea and hemp, and was involved in the woeful tale of HMS *Bounty*. Through his prolific letter writing he also swayed issues of global significance – including the colonisation of Australia.

Banks is a complex character and sometimes full of contradictions, but he exemplifies the Georgian age. To approach writing any book about Banks is to do so with some trepidation. Many authoritative biographies and books about this renowned man of science already exist and experts continue to publish thoughtful new essays about his achievements. Having read through this small celebration of his botanical achievements, I would encourage you to go on to discover more about him (see p. 124). In 2020, as we mark the bicentenary of Banks's death and prepare

for the 250th anniversary of the return of HM Bark *Endeavour* voyage in 2021, it is most certainly worth looking at Banks afresh and taking time to consider how his life has influenced many of ours today.

Sir Joseph Banks is remembered as one of the founding fathers of the Royal Botanic Gardens, Kew, with his bust displayed proudly in the reception of the Herbarium, Library and Archives building.

Banks is responsible for bringing thousands of
new plant species to British shores, including
the kaka beak (*Clianthus puniceus*) which he
first saw in New Zealand on the voyage of
HM Bark *Endeavour* (see p.27).

A botanical awakening

To say that Joseph Banks led a charmed and privileged life is probably an understatement. He was born on 15 February 1743 into a wealthy family, whose seat at Revesby Abbey in Lincolnshire numbered as just one of their estates. The Banks family was relatively new in its wealth, having risen from being yeoman farmers around the delightfully named town of Giggleswick in Yorkshire. Joseph's father, William, devoted his life to improving the family estates, but also became a Member of Parliament and deputy-lieutenant (magistrate) for Lincolnshire.

Joseph was the first of his family to receive a 'gentleman's education'. At first, he benefited from a free and easy schooling with private tutors at home, where he spent plenty of time outdoors enjoying the estate and fishing. But at the age of nine he was sent to Harrow for more discipline and to improve his education. By all accounts this was only marginally successful, and he was described as 'an active boy' with little time for his books. At 13 he was moved to Eton, which, at the time, was described as not being for those of a 'gentle disposition', but Banks was lucky in his friends and tutors. He owed much of his education to one assistant master named Edward Young, although

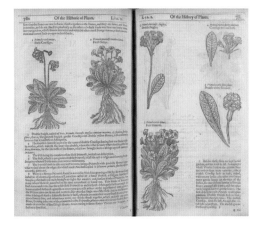

Banks reputedly found his mother's copy of John Gerard's *The Herball* or *Generall Historie of Plantes* in 1757. This was the best-known and used botany book in the country in the 17th century, and is still in print today. This edition from 1597 is held in Kew's library.

even he described Banks as having 'a great Inattention in Him, and an immediate Love of Play'.

Although not academic, Banks describes how at the age of 14 he had a revelation one day, suddenly noticing the beauty of the wildflowers around him on a walk by the Thames. He quickly became passionate about botany. On a visit home he discovered his mother's copy of Gerard's *Herball* (first published in 1597) and took it back to school with him. He was soon learning all the names of local plants and creating his own herbarium. This moment was the beginning of a lifelong botanical obsession. One of his biographers, Patrick O'Brian, says 'had it not been for botany his mind might never have blossomed at all'. At Eton, Banks also made one particular friend who would go on to have a great influence on his future – Constantine Phipps (see p. 13).

In 1760, Banks attended the University of Oxford as a 'gentleman-commoner'. He worked hard to learn natural philosophy and botany, even hiring Israel Lyons from Cambridge to teach a course in botany in 1764. Banks's commitment to his studies was admirable, especially as in 1761 his father died at the age of just 42. While many young men would have headed home or begun to dig into their newly found wealth, Banks continued his studies and made use of his mother's house in Chelsea to visit the celebrated gardener Philip Miller at the Chelsea Physic Garden and to gain botanical knowledge from William Hudson, author of *Flora Anglica*, published in 1762 – a book which became one of Banks's constant companions.

At 21, Banks's inheritance gave him estates in four counties and a yearly income of £6,000 (equivalent to over a

Banks would have been familiar with wildflowers such as the snake's head fritillary (*Fritillaria meleagris*). This illustration from *Phytanthoza iconographia* by Johann Wilhelm Weinmann in Kew's library dates to 1739.

million pounds today). After Oxford, he moved to London and joined a new circle of intellectual and influential people, formed in and around the British Museum. It was here that Banks first met the botanist Daniel Solander, with whom he would soon share many adventures.

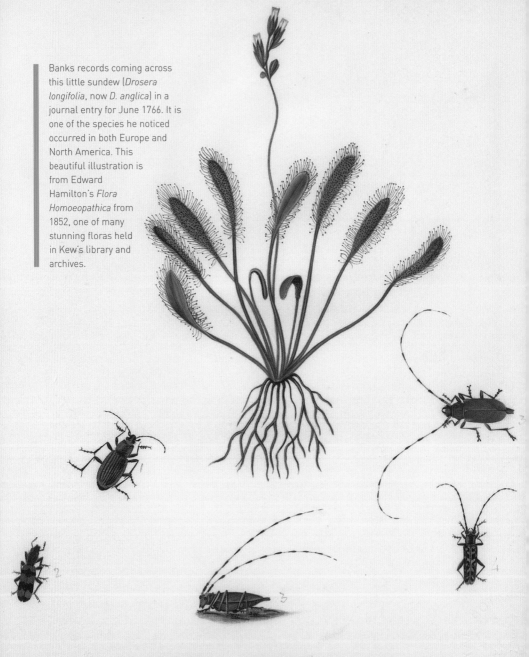

Banks records coming across this little sundew (*Drosera longifolia*, now *D. anglica*) in a journal entry for June 1766. It is one of the species he noticed occurred in both Europe and North America. This beautiful illustration is from Edward Hamilton's *Flora Homoeopathica* from 1852, one of many stunning floras held in Kew's library and archives.

Drosera longifolia.

Heading into the unknown

Instead of heading off on a Grand Tour of Europe, as many young gentlemen of means did, Banks decided he would much prefer a grand botanical tour of Labrador and Newfoundland. So, aged 22, he bought himself passage on HMS *Niger* under the command of Sir Thomas Adams, and sailed alongside his close friend Constantine Phipps, also an eager naturalist. He delighted in observing, recording and collecting plants, birds and animals there and brought home a huge number of plant specimens, including lichens and mosses, noting which he thought were similar to those which grew in England. He was the first to publish Linnaean descriptions of plants from Newfoundland. In total, he returned with records and specimens of around 340 plant species. He later catalogued almost 300 of these with details of their location and habitat, and he asked the famous botanical illustrator Georg Dionysius Ehret to immortalise 23 of them on vellum. Alongside the beginnings of an impressive herbarium, he came home with a greater determination to learn more and a reputation for zeal and focus.

Before he even returned, Banks was elected to the Royal Society. 'His election was an act of faith and hope based not on evidence of scientific performance but the incipient glint of a keen intelligence,' says his biographer H. B. Carter. That faith was to pay off way beyond everyone's expectations.

Banks collected specimens of *Kalmia polifolia* (recorded as *glauca*) while at Croque Harbour, Newfoundland. He noted in this diary 'Weather today Extreemly [sic] Hot walk out in the Evening find...Kalmia...in prodigious abundance'. Banks introduced this species to Britain, bringing it to Kew in 1767. This painting, in the first edition of *Hortus kewensis* (1789), is based on Ehret's original for Banks.

The voyage of the *Endeavour*
Setting sail

After returning from Newfoundland and Labrador, and being elected a Fellow of the Royal Society, Banks busied himself organising his expanding collections of plants and keeping informed of new botanical works and expeditions. He became great friends with Daniel Solander, a botanist at the British Museum who had studied under the great Carl Linnaeus (considered the 'father of botany' and whose system for naming plants Banks was using).

In 1768, when Banks heard of the British Admiralty's expedition under Lieutenant James Cook to study the transit of Venus, he requested places on the ship for himself and others in the hope of undertaking a thorough exploration of the natural history of the Pacific.

Banks is said to have briefly met Cook in Newfoundland, but we don't know how well they knew each other before setting sail. With the backing of the Royal Society, Banks secured nine places (at his own expense) on HM Bark *Endeavour,* and determined to take Solander with him as an expert, along with the naturalist Herman Spöring and two artists, Sydney Parkinson and

DANIEL CHARLES SOLANDER M.D.

From a Painting in the rooms of the Linnean Society

Daniel Solander was a pupil of the famous Swedish botanist Carl Linnaeus. Solander worked at the British Museum, successfully cataloguing many of their botanical specimens. He was befriended by Banks, who greatly valued his expertise and companionship.

Alexander Buchan (to record their discoveries), and four servants. Banks spent a considerable sum (around £10,000) in preparation for this expedition of a lifetime: 'no people ever went to sea better fitted out for the purpose of Natural History, nor more elegantly,' said one friend in a letter to Linnaeus at the time. A foldable, half-upholstered 'naval campaign chair',

HM Bark *Endeavour* sailed from Plymouth in August 1768, and reached Australia in 1770. This painting by Samuel Atkins depicts the moment when the *Endeavour* grounded on the Great Barrier Reef in 1770 (see p. 31).
Wikimedia Commons

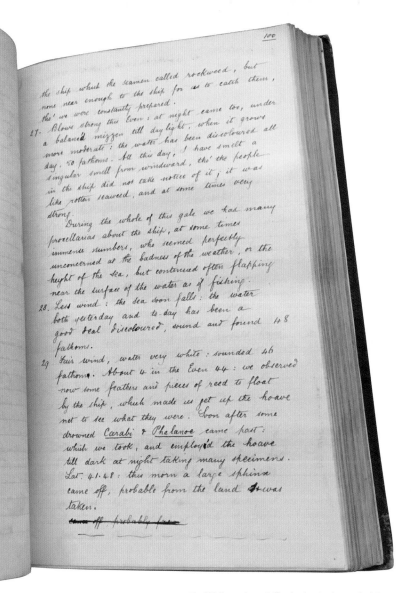

the ship which the seamen called rockweed, but
none near enough to the ship for us to catch them,
tho' we were constantly prepared.

27. Blows strong this Even: at night came too, under
a balancd mizzen till daylight, when it grows
more moderate: the water has been discoloured all
day. 50 fathoms. All this day, I have smelt a
singular smell from windward, tho' the people
in the ship did not take notice of it; it was
like rotten seaweed, and at some times very
strong.

During the whole of this gale we had many
procellarias about the ship, at some times
immense numbers, who seemed perfectly
unconcerned at the badness of the weather, or the
height of the sea, but continued often flapping
near the surface of the water as if fishing.

28. Less wind: the sea soon falls: the water
both yesterday and to-day has been a
good deal discoloured, sound and found 48
fathoms.

29. Fair wind, water very white: sounded 46
fathoms. About 4 in the Even 44: we observed
now some feathers and pieces of reed to float
by the ship, which made us get up the hoave
net to see what they were. Soon after some
drowned <u>Carabi</u> & <u>Phalanoe</u> came past:
which we took, and employ'd the hoave
till dark at night taking many specimens.
Lat. 41.48: this morn a large sphinx
came off, probable from the land & was
taken.

~~came off probably from~~

While on board, Banks kept a journal of the
voyage, recording all of the plants, places and
people he came across. Manuscript copies of
these important journals can be found in
Kew's library and archives.

thought to be the one Banks took on board and used while working in the Great Cabin, still exists at Kew today.

On 16 August 1768, Banks and Solander set off together for Plymouth to meet the *Endeavour* and begin one of history's most important and famous voyages. As we now know, this expedition was not only to observe the transit of Venus, and thereby aid future navigation, but also to explore the lands of the Southern Ocean and try to claim the 'great southern continent' for the King. It would also provide some of the most important botanical finds of that century.

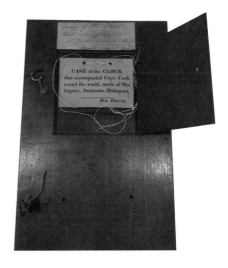

One slightly mysterious item held at Kew is Captain Cook's clock case from the *Endeavour*. It is presumed that Kew has this due to interest in the timber it is made from (mahogany), but little is known about it or the clock it once contained. Cook did not have a chronometer on board his first voyage and had to work out his longitude using the stars and a sextant – a far more error-prone method.

← This upholstered naval campaign chair, in Kew's collections, belonged to Banks and is thought to be the one he took with him on the *Endeavour*, providing comfort for the many hours spent studying and recording new plant species.

South America

Having set sail on a fair wind from Plymouth on 25 August 1768, the *Endeavour* headed towards Madeira and the Canary Islands, and then across the Atlantic towards South America. Banks noted as much marine life as he could, but eagerly awaited landfall in Rio de Janeiro to start botanising. He was to be frustrated however, as upon arrival on 13 November, and after scanning the palm-fringed shores, they were denied official permission to come ashore. The local viceroy is said to have disbelieved

The verdant flora around Rio de Janeiro was so tempting that Banks defied the viceroy and slipped ashore at night to discover as many new plants as he could. This painting from Kew's collection, by the intrepid Victorian artist Marianne North, shows the Bay of Rio and Sugar Loaf Mountain in 1873.

their story as to why they were there and thought them spies. A guard ship was placed next to the *Endeavour* and they were only allowed to restock their stores.

Banks, never one to be thwarted in his botanical ambitions, sent others ashore to collect plants for him (often leaving the ship at midnight via a cabin window and descending into a waiting boat) and once, under cover of darkness, he slipped ashore himself for a whole day. He was fascinated by the 'parasitick plants...*Malpigias, Bannisterias, Pasifloras*, not to Forget *Poinciana* and *Mimosa sensitiva* and a beatifull species of *Clutia*,' and was delighted by the variety of bromeliads, including *Bromelia karatas*. Upon leaving the harbour on 7 December, they immediately stopped at an island called Raza to investigate the plants and worked all day in the heat to collect as much as they could, including *Alstroemeria salsilla* (now known as *Bomarea salsilla*, see right).

For each specimen they carefully collected, Banks and Solander created a paper label with its name, as far they could identify it, and if it was thought to be new to science they gave it to Sydney Parkinson to draw. Considering how little access they had to the wonders of Brazil their collection of 300 species was impressive, and included some plants we are very familiar with today, such as *Bougainvillea spectabilis*.

There were no more opportunities for plant collecting until they reached Tierra

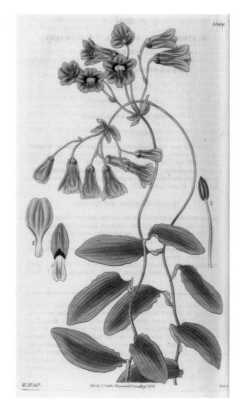

Bomarea salsilla: This elegant, climbing perennial is a native of South America and has edible roots. Its pink and green flowers are spotted with brown but can be very variable in colour. This painting by S. T. Edwards from *Curtis's Botanical Magazine* dates from 1814.

del Fuego, where they managed to gather over a hundred species and see specimens of southern beech trees (*Nothofagus*). On 20 January 1769, the *Endeavour* rounded the tip of South America and headed into the largely unknown waters of the Pacific, headed for the Society Islands and Tahiti.

Cattleya crispa: This beautiful, epiphytic, free-flowering orchid is native to the mountains above Rio de Janeiro, and is renowned for its petals' ruffled edges. It became one of the favourite orchids to grow in Britain during the early 19th century. This hand-coloured lithograph is from the portfolio 'Brazilian flowers drawn from nature in the years 1880-1882 in the neighbourhood of Rio de Janeiro: viz Larangeiras, Tijuca, Paqueta, Petropolis, many of the specimens gathered in primeval forests' by Edith Holland Norton held at Kew.

→ **Bromelia karatas:** This widespread, tall bromeliad grows on the ground and produces oblong pink edible fruits. Banks recognised the plant through having previously studied a drawing of it, and was pleased to see it in fruit. This illustration is from Kew's copy of Pierre Joseph Redouté's *Les Liliacées*, vol. 8, published in 1816.

Bromelia karatas.

Ananas karatas.

Tahiti, the Society Islands

The *Endeavour* reached the volcanic black sandy shores of Matavai Bay, Tahiti (or 'Otaheite' as Banks called it) on 13 April 1769, in preparation for their transit of Venus observations on 3 June. He described it as 'the truest picture of an Arcadia' he had ever seen. The affable young Banks quickly made genuine friendships with the Tahitians, trying to learn their language and culture, and ingratiating himself with the local queen Oborea, not to mention many of the women around her. His friendship with a high ranking 'wise man' or priest named Tupaia, who taught him Tahitian words and showed him native plants, became invaluable to the expedition as a whole. Banks acted as chief diplomat and was the first person to document Tahitian culture in detail.

The island was plentiful in coconuts, breadfruit, pandans, yams, taro, different species of banana, and fruits that 'looked like apples' but 'tasted better' – possibly the 'June plum' *Spondias dulcis* – all of which were bartered for objects such as nails, knives and beads. Banks botanised along the coastline and inland, and completed a circumnavigation of the

Kew's Economic Botany Collection contains over 90,000 plant-related objects, including over 100 pieces of tapa. This example from New Zealand's Te Papa museum, shows a 19th century highly decorated piece of tapa from Samoa.

Wikimedia Commons

N.º 6.

Many westernised engravings of Tahiti were published after the *Endeavour* voyage, including this one from Kew's copy of John Hawkesworth's account, published in 1773. The scene includes a screw pine (*Pandanus tectorius*), of which all parts were used: leaves for weaving baskets, mats and roofing; fruits for eating; flowers for making perfume and for necklaces and crowns; and timber for making canoes, weapons or housing. The roots were also used in traditional medicine.

island with Cook. He also collected objects including tapa or barkcloth, made from the inner bark of the paper mulberry (*Broussonetia papyrifera*) or the breadfruit tree (*Artocarpus altilis*). On one occasion he was given a large swathe of tapa 11 yards (approximately 10 metres) long in exchange for his silk neckerchief and a linen handkerchief.

Banks was fascinated by the breadfruit tree, or 'uru', noting how its fruit was baked or steamed before being eaten, its leaves were used for wrapping food, its bark for making cloth, its trunks for timber, and its resin for sealing canoes. He could see that it was easily propagated and cultivated, and this knowledge was to prove interesting to others back in Britain (see p. 70).

← The Otaheite plum or June plum (*Spondias dulcis*) is a widely grown tropical fruit tree. When fully ripe its flesh is beautifully sweet. Banks noted it for its usefulness, and it was later taken with breadfruit to the West Indies. This watercolour illustration is one of over 2,500 commissioned by William Roxburgh, and given to Kew in 1879.

New Zealand

It is hard for most of us to imagine the feeling of utter isolation in sailing across the vastness of the Pacific, without accurate maps, to find islands that only a few have seen before. This is, of course, what Cook and his men did with remarkable accuracy, following in the wake of Polynesian explorers who had done so hundreds of years before. Helping them sail from the Society Islands towards New Zealand was the Tahitian man Tupaia, who decided to join the expedition. Having left Tahiti in mid-July 1769, the crew sighted New Zealand on 6 October.

Cook's secondary mission was to seek out new lands and discover more of the 'great southern continent'. New Zealand at that time was practically unknown to Europeans. It had been visited briefly, and named by the Dutch navigator Abel Tasman, but its coastline and peoples were a mystery.

First contacts at Poverty Bay on the North Island were violent, with shots fired and the deaths of several Māori. This was just one of many disastrous European first meetings with the Māori, who did not hesitate to defend themselves and did not seek trade or interaction. Only Tupaia managed to defuse the situation by communicating

Banks collected many items during the *Endeavour* voyage and afterwards. Upon his return he was painted by Benjamin West dressed in a Māori cloak, surrounded by Pacific artefacts with a drawing of *Phormium tenax* at his feet.

Bridgeman Images

that they wanted to take on water and trade for food. Banks was solely focused on his botanical mission. He somehow managed to collect over 40 species of plants at Poverty Bay but looked forward to moving on in order to have the freedom to find more.

Some of their future meetings with local communities were much more successful, allowing Banks and Solander more time to botanise on land and record the astonishing flora and fauna. Among the 400 plants they collected were *Metrosideros excelsa* (now known in English as the New Zealand Christmas tree), kaka beak or glory pea (*Clianthus puniceus*), small-leaved kōwhai (*Sophora microphylla*), the white sun orchid (*Thelymitra longifolia*), the horned orchid (*Orthoceras novae-zeelandiae* – originally *O. solandri*), hebes and many ferns. The seeds Banks collected of *Sophora microphylla* and *S. tetraptera* here were some of the only viable seeds to return with him to Britain.

Banks was impressed by the beauty of New Zealand, and by what little he saw of Māori society and the expert way they cultivated crops of yams, gourds and other plants in 'gardens'. He noted in his journal finding 'many new plants', fine trees and 'very remarkable' mosses – no names were given or attempted for these species as they were so new to him. The *Endeavour* proceeded to circumnavigate New Zealand over the following months, mapping it for the first time

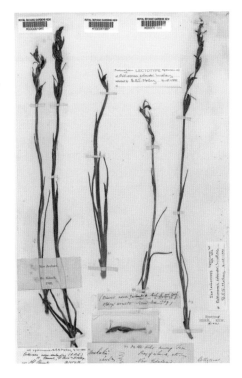

The horned orchid is endemic to the North and South Islands of New Zealand. Its green and red flowers appear between July and March. This species was originally collected by Daniel Solander on the *Endeavour* voyage to New Zealand and was subsequently named *Orthoceras solandri* after him. It is now known as *O. novae-zeelandiae*. This Kew herbarium specimen is the 'lectotype' which serves as the single specimen from which the species is described.

and confirming that it was an island and not part of a larger continent.

Banks found and collected New Zealand flax (*Phormium tenax*), known locally as *harakeke,* which was used as a source of fibre for making cordage and fishing gear, as well as clothing. He was so impressed by it that, upon his return to Britain, he posed for a portrait wearing a flax cloak (see p. 26). As in Tahiti, he also collected many cultural objects to take home.

(see p. 26)

This historic visit to New Zealand and the subsequent European colonisation of the country had many ramifications for the Māori, which are still keenly felt today. By 31 March 1770 Cook had completed his map of New Zealand, and Banks had gathered many hundreds of new plant specimens. It was time to set sail for *Terra Australis Incognita.*

Phormium was put to a great many uses by the Māori, just as pandans and coconut leaves were used by the Tahitians, including weaving its fibres into clothing, baskets and even shoes, such as this pair (left) in Kew's Economic Botany Collection. The object above shows how the fibres of the leaf can be parted using a shell and then woven into a flaxen rope.

This painting of Lake Wakatipu in New Zealand showing *Phormium* in the foreground was painted by Victorian artist Marianne North in 1881. This is just one of her 848 paintings of flora from around the world displayed in a specially commissioned 19th-century gallery at Kew.

→ Banks collected seven species of *Metrosideros* while in New Zealand on the *Endeavour* voyage. The most familiar of these today is the New Zealand Christmas tree, or pōhutukawa, (*M. excelsa*). This illustration was produced for *Curtis's Botanical Magazine* in 1850 by renowned artist W. H. Fitch.

Australia

It is probably for Cook's and Banks's arrival in Australia that the voyage of the *Endeavour* is best known. While the west and north coasts of the continent had been visited by traders and explorers before, the east coast was unknown to Europeans and unmapped. The crew sighted the coast of New South Wales on 19 April 1770 and began to sail north to chart the coast with Banks noting in his journal that 'every hill seemd to be cloth'd with trees of no mean size'. On 29 April they stopped at a natural harbour allowing Banks and Solander several days to enjoy botanising. Due to the sheer number of plants they collected (132), Cook recorded the place as Botany Bay and the two arms of the bay Point Solander and Cape Banks.

This is where they collected the first specimens of what we now see as botanical emblems of Australia, such as the saw banksia (*B. serrata*) – one of the first four species of *Banksia* recorded. Once pollinated, their nectar-filled flowers are followed by bizarre woody seed capsules or 'cones' which make them a truly distinctive group of plants. Although banksias were common trees along the eastern coast, they were so unique and beautiful that they alone were chosen to be named after Banks as

Over 170 species of *Banksia* are now known including this stunning *B. coccinea*, illustrated here by the famous botanical artist Franz Bauer (see p. 66). This original painting is held in Kew's collections.

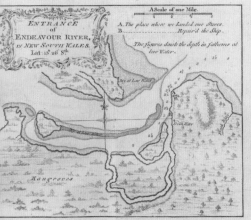

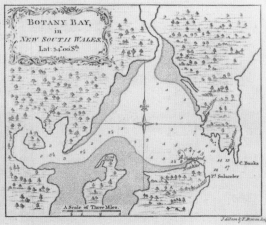

a genus (many other plants have the species name of *banksia* or *banksiae*). There are now over 170 recorded species of *Banksia* (see also p. 113).

Archaeological evidence shows that Aboriginal peoples had lived around this area for 5,000 years, and indeed the crew of the *Endeavour* saw many groups of people as they travelled up the coast. However, although Banks made notes about their encounters, their interaction was minimal, in contrast to those in New Zealand and Tahiti. As they travelled to the north-eastern tip of the country, the *Endeavour* had a mishap with the coral reef and urgent repairs had to be organised. This took several

In his account of the *Endeavour* voyage, published in 1773, John Hawkesworth included maps of both Botany Bay and the Endeavour River, where the ship anchored for repairs. Taken from an original copy held in Kew's library.

weeks, giving Banks valuable time to make extensive collections of the native flora along what Cook named the Endeavour River (known locally as Wabalumbaal), with each new species recorded in detail by Sydney Parkinson. With such a vast new collection of plants, Banks recorded in his journal that Parkinson was extremely busy making: 'in just 14 days . . . 94 sketches, so quick a hand has he.'

Plants never previously seen by European eyes continued to be gathered and recorded on an almost daily basis, including species of *Eucalyptus, Acacia, Melaleuca* and *Grevillea*. One of the few herbarium specimens made by Banks in Kew's Herbarium is that of *Melaleuca arcana* – a pretty, small tree with frothy creamy-white flowers from Far North Queensland. This is thought to have been collected at Point Lookout, north of the Endeavour River. This rare plant, like many others he recorded, is endemic to the region he collected it in – the specimen wasn't correctly identified and described at Kew until 1964!

It is hard for us to comprehend how, having been so impressed by the beauty and floral riches of the country, and knowing the area to already be occupied by indigenous people, Banks then recommended the British colonisation of Australia through the establishment of a penal colony at Botany Bay. Yet he became one of the biggest supporters of this settlement, and continued to support Australia's new governors throughout his life.

The *Endeavour* began its return journey from Australia, home to the shores of Britain, in late 1770. The journey included a stopover in Jakarta, Indonesia, for more repairs and to restock supplies. Unfortunately, this was to have fatal consequences for some of

The temperate Australian forests were to prove happy plant-hunting grounds for Banks and Solander, who collected hundreds of new species. This painting by Marianne North shows forests of tree ferns in south-east Australia.

Banks collected cultural and useful objects from all the Pacific societies he visited, including several from Australia. Kew's Economic Botany Collection holds a vast array of aboriginal artefacts similar to those that Banks amassed, including this wooden 'devil scarer'.

This Kew herbarium specimen of the rare *Melaleuca arcana* is the original one made from the specimen collected by Banks close to the Endeavour River in Queensland.

the crew, including Parkinson and Tupaia, who contracted dysentery and died. Banks, as ever, was fortunate, and returned from his adventure on 12 July 1771 with over 30,000 specimens of plants, leading to the description of 110 new genera and 1,300 new species – increasing the world's scientifically described flora by an estimated 25 per cent. He and Solander became the toast of London and of British scientific circles.

As well as his specimens and journals, Banks also had the many hundreds of drawings and watercolours by Sydney Parkinson. He set about creating a 'florilegium' and employed five artists and eighteen engravers to create 743 copperplate line engravings of his plant discoveries. Solander then spent 13 years creating botanical descriptions to accompany the artworks. Despite completing this tremendously important work, Banks never published it: the florilegium was printed for the first time between 1980 and 1990 using the original plates, which were discovered in the Natural History Museum. Kew's library houses one of the full limited edition sets.

Banks and Solander collected four species of the plants that would become known as *Banksia* on this expedition. Over 170 species are now known. This *B. aemula* is from *Forest Flora of New South Wales*, 1902-4.

→ The flora of Australia was unlike anything else seen by European eyes before. Decades later, in 1880, Victorian painter Marianne North delighted in capturing two of the iconic species of the country: *Eucalyptus marginata* and *Grevillea banksii*.

Sydney Parkinson

Described as an amiable, conscientious and highly talented young man, the 18-year-old Sydney Parkinson was a truly gifted artist. Before the *Endeavour* voyage Banks had employed him to draw some of his Newfoundland collections, and in 1767 he sent him to Kew Gardens to draw some of its plants.

On board the *Endeavour*, Parkinson documented a vast array of the scenes, people, plants, fish, birds and other animals, as well as cultural objects they came across. Banks admired him for his accuracy and speed in sketching and described him as working with 'unbounded industry'. In total, he made nearly a thousand drawings, which are an invaluable record of the voyage and its discoveries.

He worked in very difficult and often cramped conditions, dealing with rolling seas, plagues of flies, heat and damp – surely an artist's worst nightmares. Parkinson was one of two artists that Banks had brought on board, the other – a landscape artist named Alexander Buchan – unfortunately died of epilepsy shortly after arriving in Tahiti in 1769. Parkinson therefore took on the full duties of recording both landscapes and specimens, creating beautiful

After the death of Alexander Buchan, the *Endeavour*'s landscape painter, Parkinson took up the job of capturing the astonishing landscapes they encountered, as well as all the flora and fauna. This engraving, from Kew's copy of *A Journal of a Voyage to the South Seas*, portrays 'Tolago Bay' on the east coast of New Zealand.

The frontispiece of the publication of Parkinson's journals of the *Endeavour* voyage includes this rare portrait of the young artist.

picturesque drawings as well as iconic botanical art. He is noted as the first European artist to visit Australia and New Zealand.

Parkinson kept his own unassuming and readable journal of the voyage and its discoveries, but sadly he never made it home. On 26 January 1771 he died of dysentery on board the *Endeavour*, as did several others, while sailing through the Indian Ocean en route home. Of the eight people Banks took on board the ship, only two survived the whole journey.

The journal was later published by Sydney's brother Stanfield as *A Journal of a Voyage to the South Seas*. Stanfield clearly felt slighted by Banks and published an uncompromising view of him in the book's introduction. Although Banks did not offer Stanfield much time, he did pay him all of Sydney's wages due from the voyage and an extra £500 in light of his lasting gratitude to Sydney.

Meeting the monarch

King George III had taken a keen interest in the adventures of the *Endeavour* and the fascinating botanical discoveries that had been made. On 10 August 1771, Banks and Solander were presented to the King and Queen at Kew Gardens. They obviously made a good impression, as the King soon began to ask Banks's advice on the gardens. By 1773, Banks had created an unofficial role for himself as 'a kind of superintendence over his Royal Botanic Gardens.'

Banks had expected to join Cook on his second voyage, to find the mythical southern continent (Antarctica). However, disputes over details of accommodation and how much Banks could bring on board led him to pull out in a fit of pique, and instead plan his own expedition – to the Hebrides and Iceland. It is probably no coincidence that the two voyages left on the same day of 12 July 1772. The choice of Iceland was linked to the then fashionable interest in volcanoes and the fact the country had been so little explored by other botanists. The expedition lasted for just six weeks, and he returned from this, his final, voyage with hundreds more new illustrations and specimens.

His Majesty, George 3rd

King George III inherited both the Kew and Richmond gardens, and determined to continue his mother's work in developing the botanic garden.

Wellcome Collection

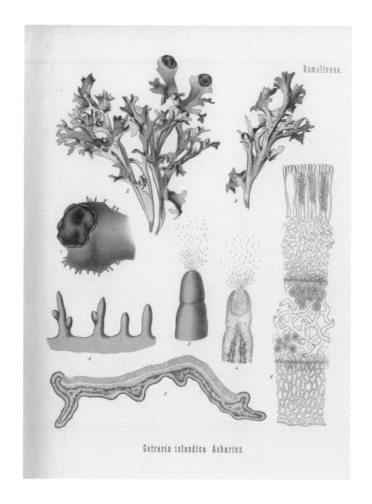

Ramalineae.

Cetraria islandica Acharius.

Banks collected a range of lichens in Iceland including this *Cetraria islandica*. This coloured plate labelled 'Cetraria islandica acharius' is from Köhler's *Medizinal-Pflanzen*, Vol. 2, 1887 in Kew's library.

W.^m & Marlow delin.^t

A View of the Lake and Island at Kew, seen from the with the Bridge, the Temples of Arethusa, and Victory, and the Great Pagoda.

The royal gardens at Kew had been mainly laid out by George's parents Prince Frederick and Princess Augusta, as a landscape garden full of follies and interesting trees, with an eleven-acre botanic garden and arboretum off to one side. King George and Banks determined to expand this with plants from all over the world. This view of the early landscape gardens at Kew, looking towards the Pagoda, is from Sir William Chambers' *Plans of the Gardens...at Kew*, 1763.

P. Sandby sculp.

Despite all of his experience and vast collections, Banks never published any of his discoveries himself. Instead, he opened up his unrivalled collections to other scientists and delighted in sharing his knowledge. His house at 32 Soho Square in London – equipped with a large herbarium and an exceptional scientific library open to any *bona fide* researcher – became a meeting place for scientists and botanists.

Kew became an extension of this authority and research. Banks would meet the King at Kew on Saturdays, walking the whole estate and discussing its improvement, as well as new developments in agriculture. It was Banks and one of Kew's head gardeners, William Aiton, who really determined that Kew would become a true 'botanic garden' with a clear focus on plants of use to the British Empire. They followed in the footsteps of Princess Augusta and Lord Bute (described as one of the foremost botanists in Britain) who had begun the 'Exotick Garden' at Kew in 1760 and had already built up an interesting plant collection.

Many plants were already sent as gifts to Kew and the King when, in 1772, Banks advised the King to begin sending out his own plant collectors on purposeful missions, to ensure the new royal collection would be unrivalled across the world (see p. 50). Banks often insisted that 'as many new plants as possible should make their first appearance at the

Royal Gardens.' Its borders and glasshouses soon began to burgeon with new discoveries. Banks immediately instigated a new programme of plant labelling – switching from an unwieldy number and catalogue system to one where all plants had their own labels with their full Latin name. This common-sense approach proved to be an invaluable system and continues to this day.

King George III's new and expanded botanic garden was not just a hobby; it was a statement of royal authority and political sway. The discovery of new plants, and holding species that others did not have, gave the King and Great Britain an advantage and became a source of diplomatic power. Rare plants were shared as gifts with other royal courts. Having the best gardens and plant collections that displayed the wealth of your empire was a matter of some serious competition in Europe at the time. King George was determined that his garden was to be the most beautiful, diverse and useful.

From being an interested amateur, and then a serious naturalist and collector, Banks now became one of the most influential men of botany in the world. Through the 1780s he worked diligently with Aiton and others at Kew to expand the collections and to plant many hundreds of trees, particularly from North America. Together, Banks, Aiton and the botanists Solander and Jonas Dryander created a verified list of all the plants growing in the new botanic garden. This was published in three volumes as *Hortus Kewensis* in 1789, containing an astonishing 5,600 species, complete with details of their introductions. It has become one of the most important records in British horticultural history (see p. 48).

Such was the strength of Banks's reputation, based on his expeditions and his work at Kew, that in 1774, at the age of just 35, he was elected president of the Royal Society. These two institutions and the advancement of science were to occupy the rest of his life.

As this 1771 map from Kew's library and archives shows, at this time Kew was still two royal landscaped estates. The small botanic garden existed at the north end of the Kew garden (shown here at far right of the map). King George did not combine the gardens until 1802.

The development of Kew's gardens

The 18th century was a truly fascinating time to be a gardener and a botanist. With royal and national support, new plants – never seen or grown before in Britain – were arriving from all over the world. Hundreds of new species were received from North America, and many voyages were setting off with the purpose of discovery, complete with naturalists and artists on board.

When the young gardener William Aiton came to Kew in 1759 it was mainly a pleasure garden, tastefully landscaped with walks and follies. But accounts show that by the early 1760s he was in charge of the small new 'Physick Garden'. Having trained under Banks's friend and mentor, Philip Miller of the Chelsea Physic Garden, Aiton was described as being 'the most competent man in England where tropical and sub-tropical plants were concerned'. Aiton's superior skills in horticulture helped to grow Kew's reputation, as he was 'a perfect master of his business.'

Aiton initially worked with the talented and knowledgeable Lord Bute to develop an eleven-acre botanic garden at the north end of the pleasure grounds, near the Orangery, which included a five-acre arboretum of rare trees (a handful of which still survive today as

William Aiton, who helped the early gardens at Kew to thrive, is pictured here holding *Aitonia capensis* (now called *Nymania capensis*), also known as Chinese lantern, a South African shrub named after him by Carl Thunberg. This oil painting, once believed to be by Johann Zoffany but now attributed to Edmund Bristow, is held in Kew's art collections. You can see Aiton's tomb in the cemetery at St Anne's Church on Kew Green alongside many other luminaries.

A View of the Palace at Kew belonging to her Royal Highness the Princess Dowager of Wales.

This engraving of the Kew landscape in 1763, by architect Sir William Chambers, shows the White House (now sadly gone) where the royal family lived while at Kew. To the right is the Orangery and the original botanic garden and arboretum.

the Old Lions). While Banks is often cited as the first unofficial director of Kew, this title could very easily also be applied to Bute, and Kew was already a garden of note by the time Banks became involved.

The royals' interest in botany brought gifts of new plants to the gardens but many also arrived from commercial plant distributors, and nurserymen, including James Gordon and Lee & Kennedy, who were introducing new plants of their own. By the late 1760s Kew already had a list of 3,400 species.

Aiton had first met Banks in 1764 and had allowed Sydney Parkinson to come to Kew to draw flowers for Banks in 1767. When Banks took over supervision of the gardens there was a smooth transition, and Banks and Aiton developed a good working relationship. Early on, in 1773, Banks had Kew staff planting thousands of trees from 800 different species. And Banks's advice, in 1772, to hire a plant collector to head to the Cape in South Africa (see p. 53) soon had myriad exotic new species flooding back to Aiton's hands.

Aiton placed many of these in the Great Stove – an early 'glasshouse' (designed by architect Sir William Chambers and erected in 1761) heated by flues beneath the floor and in the walls, and in some sections by rotting bark. The Stove, which faced out onto the Exotic or Botanic Garden, contained succulents, palms, African bulbs and tender annuals

among many other plants. At 114 ft long (almost 35 metres), it was one of the largest conservatories in the country and a great responsibility.

Aiton's botanical talents allowed Bute's and Banks's visions of a global plant collection to thrive, and Kew was truly beginning to flourish.

This stunning bulb (now named *Boophone disticha*) from the Cape was imported to Kew by Francis Masson around 1774, and is typical of the stunning rarities he sent to the gardens. This original illustration for *Curtis's Botanical Magazine*, held in Kew's collections, dates from 1809.

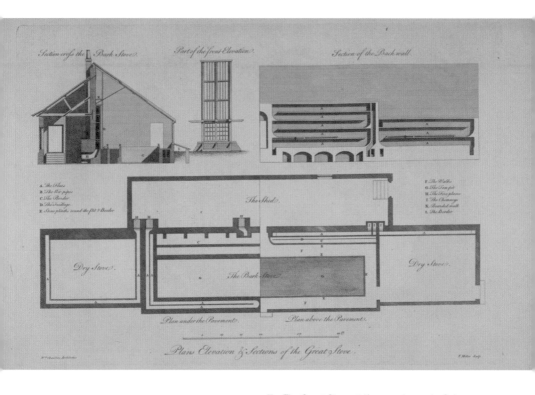

The Great Stove at Kew was begun by Prince Frederick and completed in 1761. Designed by Sir William Chambers and the Reverend Stephen Hales, it held some of the most important and unusual plants in the country at the time. This plate of the plans for the Great Stove at Kew, from Chambers' *Plans; elevations; sections and perspective views of the gardens and buildings at Kew in Surrey; the seat of Her Royal Highness the Princess Dowager of Wales*, 1763, is held in Kew's library.

Writing horticultural history

William Aiton will long be remembered at Kew for one book – or rather a series of volumes, which have since become touchstones of horticultural history. First published in August 1789, his *Hortus Kewensis* is a three-volume list of all the plants that were growing at Kew at that time (5,600 species), complete with botanical descriptions and dates of introduction.

Aiton is credited as the book's author and 'gardener to his Majesty', although Jonas Dryander and others were responsible for all the brief botanical descriptions. In its dedication to the King however, Aiton writes: 'Small as the book appears, the composition of it has cost him a large portion of the leisure allowed by the daily duties of his station, during more than sixteen years'. The book is a time capsule of knowledge of what plants were in Britain at the time.

The first edition in Kew's library includes illustrations by Banks's engraver Daniel Mackenzie, who took drawings by Ehret, Sowerby and other noted artists and created coloured engravings for these volumes, under Banks's supervision. One such is that of the swamp orchid, *Limodorum tankervilleae* (now *Phaius tankervilleae*), named by Banks after Lady Emma Tankerville, a

Aiton's *Hortus Kewensis* (1789) comes in three volumes. This first edition in Kew's library is a piece of horticultural history.

wealthy plant collector who lived in Walton-on-Thames, who had managed to get this species to flower.

Aiton's *Hortus Kewensis* was not a one-off – new volumes continued to be published – nor was it the first, as botanist John Hill had created a much earlier version in 1768 listing 3,400 species. The second Aiton edition in five volumes was completed by Aiton's son, W. T. Aiton, between 1810 and 1813. The tradition of documenting all the plants at Kew continued through the

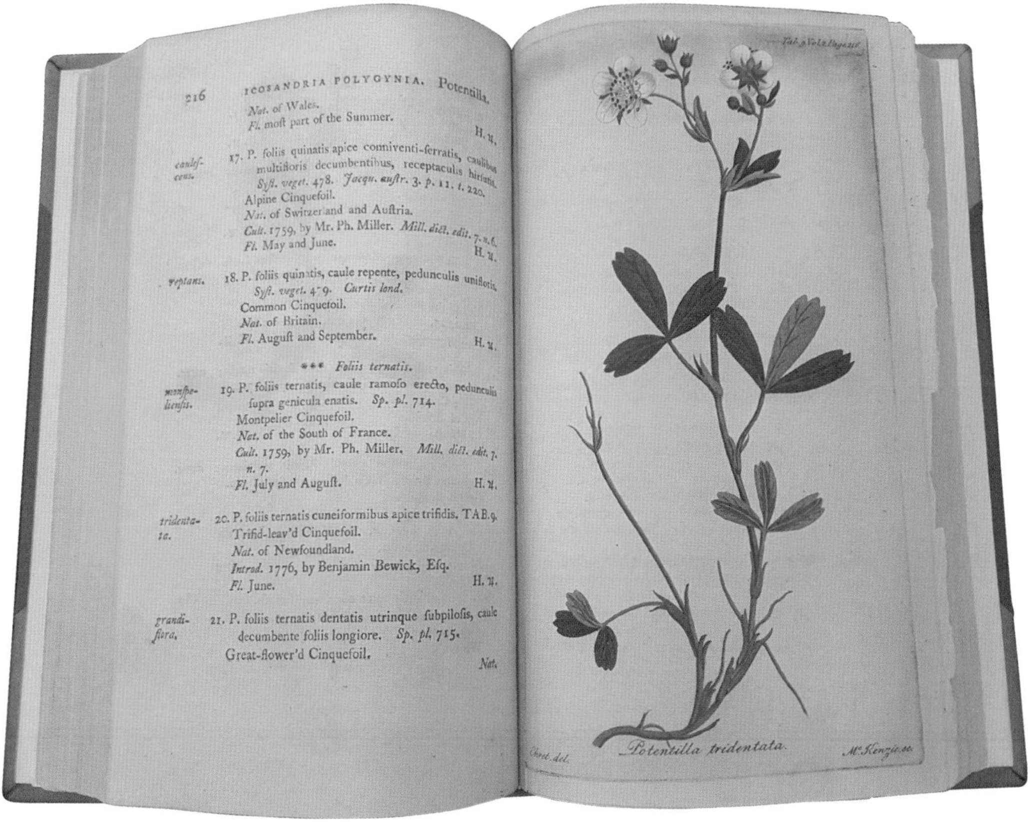
216 ICOSANDRIA POLYGYNIA. Potentilla.
Nat. of Wales.
Fl. moſt part of the Summer. H. ♃.
caulescens. 17. P. foliis quinatis apice conniventi-ſerratis, caulibus multifloris decumbentibus, receptaculis hirſutis. Syſt. veget. 478. Jacqu. auſtr. 3. p. 11. t. 220.
Alpine Cinquefoil.
Nat. of Switzerland and Auſtria.
Cult. 1759, by Mr. Ph. Miller. Mill. dict. edit. 7. n. 6.
Fl. May and June. H. ♃.
reptans. 18. P. foliis quinatis, caule repente, pedunculis unifloris. Syſt. veget. 479. Curtis lond.
Common Cinquefoil.
Nat. of Britain.
Fl. Auguſt and September. H. ♃.
*** Foliis ternatis.
monſpeliensis. 19. P. foliis ternatis, caule ramoſo erecto, pedunculis ſupra genicula enatis. Sp. pl. 714.
Montpelier Cinquefoil.
Nat. of the South of France.
Cult. 1759, by Mr. Ph. Miller. Mill. dict. edit. 7. n. 7.
Fl. July and Auguſt. H. ♃.
tridentata. 20. P. foliis ternatis cuneiformibus apice trifidis. TAB. 9.
Trifid-leav'd Cinquefoil.
Nat. of Newfoundland.
Introd. 1776, by Benjamin Bewick, Eſq.
Fl. June. H. ♃.
grandiflora. 21. P. foliis ternatis dentatis utrinque ſubpiloſis, caule decumbente foliis longiore. Sp. pl. 715.
Great-flower'd Cinquefoil.
Nat.
Potentilla tridentata.

19th century and was even supported by a legacy in Charles Darwin's will. Today, the idea still lives on and such documentation of plants is now available online via the International Plant Names Index and other such databases.

Only a few images are included in the first edition of *Hortus Kewensis*, including this painting of *Potentilla tridentata* (now *Sibbaldia tridentata*).

Plant hunting for Kew

Banks had a grand vision for the King's garden – for it to be the best botanic garden in the world, where plants from around the globe could be brought, grown and then used for the expansion of the British Empire. He wanted to make Kew unique. To this end, Banks persuaded the King of the merits of sending out his own plant collectors.

Banks wanted loyal men, who would take direction without question, with a knowledge of gardening and botany and a real streak of ambition. He not only wanted the collectors to find new and interesting plants, but to bring back information on how they could be grown and what they could be used for.

Banks focused on South Africa, Australia and South America – areas he personally knew contained floral riches which might also be grown outside at Kew. Banks reportedly gave each collector a thorough briefing before they left – on the correct ways of collecting, drying, recording, labelling, packing or growing on seeds and plants to be shipped back to Britain, and how to prevent them suffering from salt spray on board (see p. 74).

There is no denying that plant hunting was a dangerous affair. These men often travelled with little money, help,

Plant collectors often took a variety of equipment with them including a 'vasculum' (usually made of metal but sometimes leather or wood) for storing plants in as they went about their daily explorations. This wooden 19th-century example is in Kew's Economic Botany Collection.

Plant hunting could be a dangerous business and offered little financial reward, but it was an amazing chance to travel and become an expert in the botany of a region, collecting plants no European had seen before. This wood engraving from the 19th century portrays the adventures of a plant collector.

INTERFOTO / Sammlung Rauch / Mary Evans

direction or maps. Several of Kew's collectors lost their lives to shipwrecks, disease and mishap, while mutiny was also not out of the question (see p. 70). Francis Masson, Anton Hove and George Caley were the first of Kew's plant collectors and they were soon followed by Peter Good, David Nelson, Allan Cunningham, James Bowie, William Kerr and others. When Masson left England for South Africa in 1772, he began a practice of professional plant collecting in the wild for Kew that continues to this day.

It is estimated that Banks introduced over 7,000 new plant species into cultivation in Britain through his own collecting and that of his intrepid collectors.

Protea

Lee & Ken

May 2

Francis Masson heads south

If you walk through the Victorian temple of glass that is the Temperate House at Kew today, you can see a range of extraordinary plant species that were first brought to this country by the plant hunter Francis Masson.

Masson was recommended to Banks by Aiton, and Banks saw to it that the Royal Society recommended Masson to the King. Neither monarch nor Banks could have been disappointed with his work, as Masson returned from the South African Cape in 1775 with stunning proteas, bright pelargoniums and gladioli, as well as cape heaths (*Erica*), exotic members of the Iris family called *Ixia*, cycads (*Encephalartos*), aloes, and several flowering succulents, including the wonderfully weird *Stapelia* (on which Masson became an expert). Before these floral jewels were delivered, few South African plants had made it back to Europe alive.

When the *Endeavour* had stopped at Cape Town, Banks had little time to botanise as, it is thought, he had been recovering from illness after the fateful stop in Jakarta. He had glimpsed its potential for botanical delight, however, and almost everything Masson saw and collected proved to be a curious gem. At one point Masson describes the

Francis Masson (1741–1805), Kew's first official plant collector. This portrait by George Garrard is held by the Linnean Society.

← Masson collected hundreds of new species from the Cape – many of which are very familiar to us today, including proteas. This original illustration of *Protea formosa* (introduced by Masson in 1789) in Kew's collection was produced for *Curtis's Botanical Magazine*.

landscape in his journal as 'being enamelled with the greatest number of flowers I ever saw, of exquisite beauty and fragrance.'

It is widely assumed that Masson introduced the bird of paradise flower (*Strelitzia reginae*; named in honour of the King's wife, Charlotte of Mecklenburg-Strelitz) to Britain in 1773, although Aiton credited it to Banks in *Hortus Kewensis*. Masson went on to introduce other stunning species from that genus. In all, he is thought to have sent over 500 plant species from South Africa to Kew, many of which were portrayed in *Curtis's Botanical Magazine* and set off a craze for 'Cape flowers' in England.

Directed by Banks, Masson dedicated his life to plant collecting, spending time in the Azores and Canaries, West Indies, Mediterranean and North Africa, and having another much longer stay (of nine years) at the Cape, before finally heading to Canada in 1797. He stayed there until his death in 1805, aged 65, after an amazingly eventful life of plant hunting for King and country. He had changed the face of Kew and many of our gardens since (see also p. 102 and p. 120).

↑ Masson was the first to collect the bird of paradise flower *Strelitzia reginae*, named for Queen Charlotte. This stunning painting by Franz Bauer (see p. 66) is from Kew's collections.

→ Masson sent a specimen of the Eastern Cape giant cycad (*Encephalartos altensteinii*) from South Africa in 1775. It produced one cone in 1819, which Banks made a special trip to Kew to see. This plant has now been at Kew for 245 years and is often claimed to be the oldest pot plant in the world. This illustration of a cone sent to Kew in 1890 was for *Curtis's Botanical Magazine*.

½ nat size

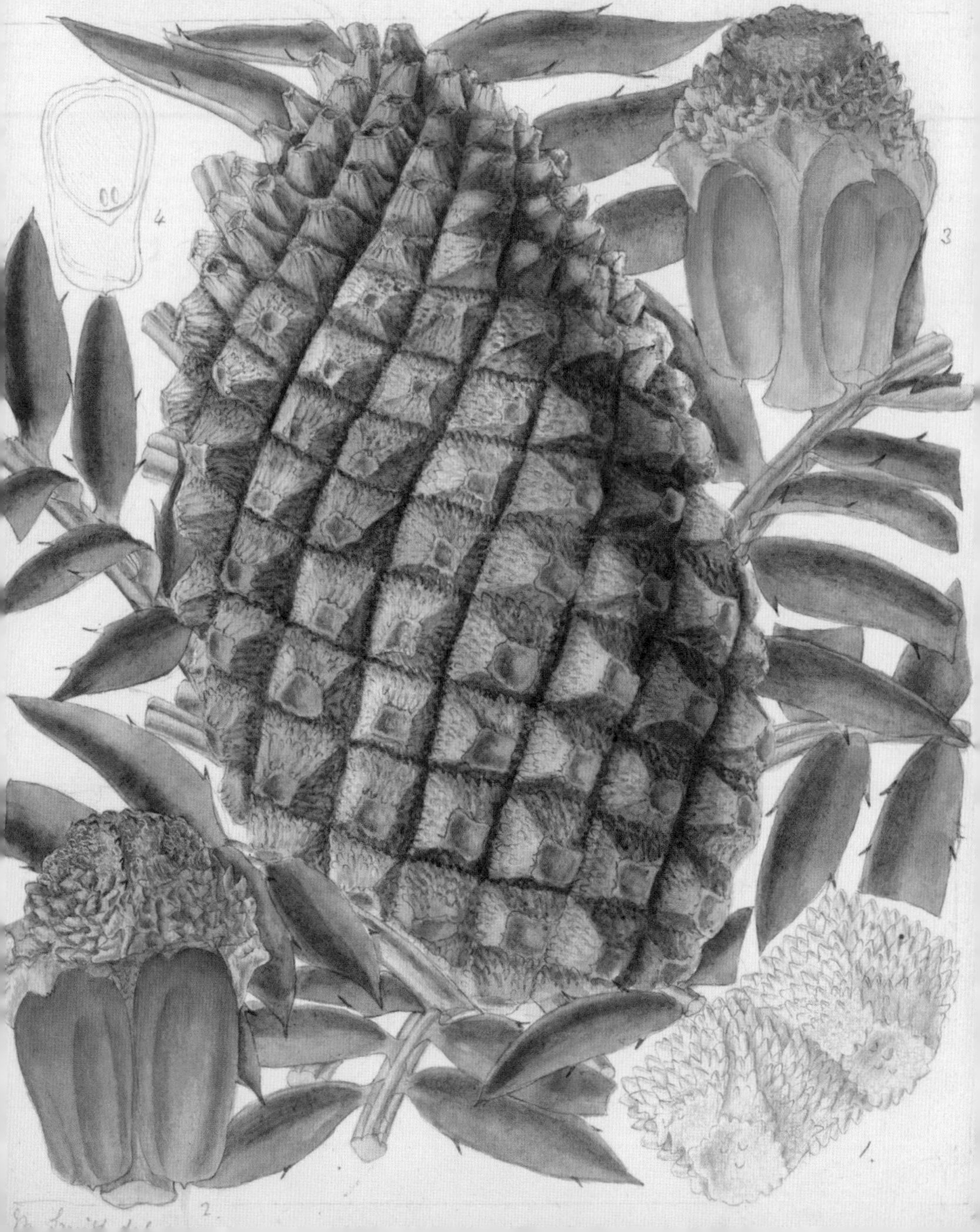

Menzies and the monkey puzzle

It was mainly due to Banks's influence on the Royal Society, and thereby the Admiralty, that naturalists and 'men of science' were nearly always placed on board official 'voyages of discovery'. Banks often recommended the people who would join these voyages. For James Cook's third voyage he put forward the surgeon William Anderson and Kew gardener-botanist David Nelson (see p. 72).

In 1791, the government decided to send out another expedition under George Vancouver, which was to last four years, taking in the Cape of Good Hope, Australia, New Zealand, Tahiti, Hawaii and Canada, and surveying the north-west coast of North America before heading to South America. Banks used his influence to install the Scottish botanist and surgeon Archibald Menzies on board. Banks charged Menzies to record as much as he could, collecting plants, animals and birds as well as items from the local peoples they encountered, and asked him for regular updates.

This was not Menzies's first visit to the Americas, having sent back seeds to Banks and Kew on previous voyages there. However, this expedition is now remembered for being the first time that many of North America's spectacular

An original letter in Kew's archives from Menzies to Banks hints at the amazing tale of the collection of monkey puzzle seeds.

The monkey puzzle is now the national tree of Chile but is classed as Endangered because its wild population is under threat from logging, deforestation and fires. Conservation efforts are underway, and many botanic gardens in the northern hemisphere that have a similar temperate rainforest climate grow monkey puzzles to preserve their genetic diversity. These striking trees were captured in this painting by Victorian painter Marianne North, held at Kew.

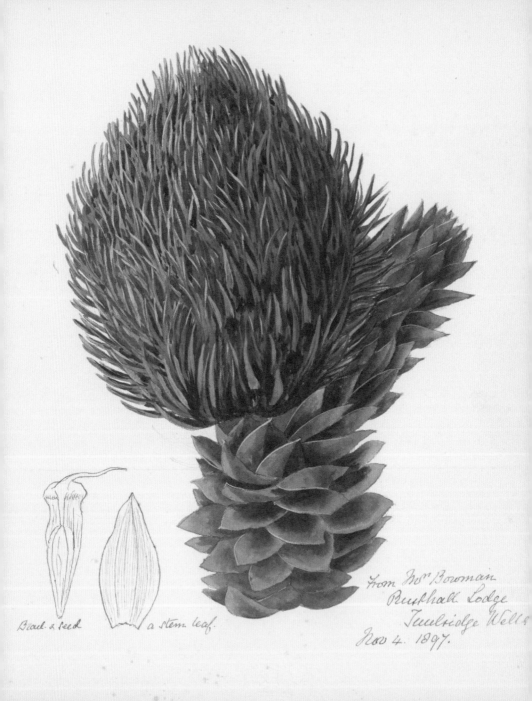

Brad. & seed.   a stem leaf.

From Mrs Bowman
Rusthall Lodge
Tunbridge Wells
Nov 4. 1897.

conifers, including the giant redwood, Douglas fir and Monterey pine, were first recorded, and most especially for the story of the monkey puzzle.

Sadly, Menzies's own journal entry for the encounter in Santiago, Chile, has been lost, but he obviously told the story frequently as it was recounted by Kew's director Sir Joseph Hooker years later. In a letter to Banks dated 28 April 1795, Menzies only gives a tantalising introduction to the tale:

> *When our arrival was made known to His Excellency O' Higgins the Presidt of Chile (an Irish Gentleman) he ordered our wants to be supplied in the most liberal manner and sent a very friendly invitation for us to visit the Capital (Santiago) in consequence of which Captain Vancouver & five of his officers, of which I had the pleasure to be one, went to visit upon him.*

> *We were treated with every mark of attention and friendly hospitality…but the particular account of this journey I must defer till I have the pleasure of seeing you.*

Vancouver and his men were invited to a banquet by Ambrosio O'Higgins. The story goes that a dessert was served which contained large seeds that Menzies did not recognise, so he pocketed some of them and later propagated them on board ship in his deck-top plant frame. Five survived the journey back to Britain. The seeds turned out to be from the large coniferous tree *Araucaria araucana*, later to be commonly known in Britain as the monkey puzzle. Of the five saplings, Banks planted one at his home in Spring Grove, Isleworth. The other four stayed at Kew; one was planted outside (near the Ice House) and three others under glass. Over the years, only the outdoors specimen at Kew survived, becoming known as 'Joseph Banks's pine'. It was often shown to visitors by King William IV and is said to have survived until 1892.

Menzies is commemorated in the name of many plants including *Menziesia*, a genus of shrubs now classed as part of the *Rhododendron* genus, the Douglas fir *Pseudotsuga menziesii*, one of the most ecologically and commercially important trees in western North America, and madrone *Arbutus menziesii*. His contribution to discovering and introducing new plants into Britain was more fully recognised once his herbarium, journals and notes were found in Banks's herbarium and library long after their deaths.

This beautiful original painting by Mary Anne Stebbing, 1897, in Kew's collection, shows the details of a female *Araucaria* cone.

Allan Cunningham in Australia

After a hiatus during the Napoleonic Wars, Banks and W. T. Aiton (William Aiton's son and successor) renewed their dedication to plant collecting. Knowing that the botanical bounty of Australia still remained largely unstudied (despite the large collections he himself had brought back) and that the continent was essentially unexplored by Europeans, Banks was keen to get collectors over to the Antipodes to discover its wonders.

With the younger Aiton's help, he selected two more Kew gardeners – James Bowie and Allan Cunningham, for their honesty, diligence and work ethic – to become plant hunters. They first travelled together to Brazil and sent back many new South American plants, including orchids and bromeliads. Having proved their worth, Banks then directed Cunningham to head to Australia, and Bowie to South Africa. They set off with orders to search for new plants that might be grown outside or in unheated conservatories at Kew.

Cunningham, born in the quiet village of Wimbledon to a Scottish head gardener father, was to become Australia's most prolific plant collector of the early 19th century, and an indefatigable explorer, as can be seen

Allan Cunningham was just one of Kew's Australian collectors, but by far the most prolific and successful. He continued to collect for Kew even after Banks's death. This informal crayon portrait by Sir Daniel Macnee is held in Kew's archives.

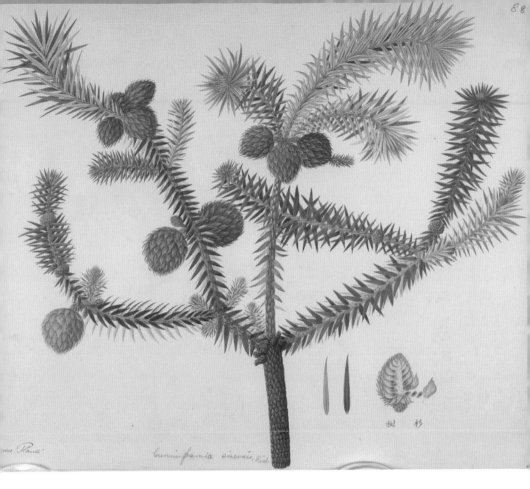

Cunninghamia sinensis, Rich.

树杉

from the effect he had on Australia's maps and place names. He arrived in 1816, and notably travelled through the Blue Mountains in 1817 collecting over 400 plants. He circumnavigated the continent in 1819 on board HMS *Mermaid* with Captain Phillip Parker King, after which he sent four cases of plants back to Kew. He retraced Banks's steps to the Endeavour River in Queensland and also opened up a new

The conifer genus *Cunninghamia* is named in honour of this intrepid explorer. This original painting of the China fir, *Cunninghamia lanceolata* (syn. *C. sinensis*), is from the Kew Kerr Chinese collection.

route through the Great Dividing Range to the Darling Downs, now known as Cunningham's Gap (now part of the Main Range National Park). Kew's 'Inwards' books are full of handwritten records of plants received from Cunningham over the years – including trees, shrubs, tree ferns and many orchids.

In 1814, at the beginning of his career, Cunningham wrote to Banks:

It is a love of plants and to search for them in their wild state, and a wish to make myself useful in the capacity of a collector . . . it shall be the highest ambition of my life to exert myself in the perform[ance] of the requisite duties that constitute a collector, so that the Royal collection at Kew may exceed all other collections in the riches of new, beautiful and desirable plants.

A long letter to Banks dated 8 November 1819, in Kew's archives, gives an overview of his journey on the *Mermaid*, which offered him 'favourable opportunity . . . for Botanical Investigation'. He notes where he followed in the wake of Cook and Banks, and then the botanist Robert Brown (see p. 116). He mentions collections and sightings of *Banksia, Sophora* and *Grevillea*, as well as other shrubs, plants and bulbs, and notes the similarities of plants in certain areas to those in Asia. Banks must have appreciated the way that in this letter Cunningham helped him relive his own

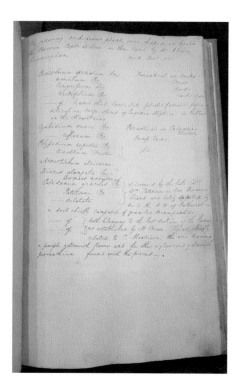

Cunningham sent many hundreds of plants to Kew during his years as a plant collector, all of which are recorded in Kew's 'Inwards Books'.

experiences of adventure: 'You may with pleasure, call to remembrance . . . the beautiful blueish flowering Nymphaea expanding its flowers and leaves on the surface of the chains of stagnant pools in the lower land'.

In return, Banks's last letter to Cunningham, in 1820, was full of praise: 'the Royal Gardens have materially benefited by what we had from you. I write you a short letter because I am not well . . . I entirely approve of the whole of your conduct, as does also our worthy friend, Aiton at Kew.'

Although Cunningham proved to be the last of Banks's plant collectors, he continued collecting for Kew and exploring the continent after Banks's death, and developed a strong relationship with Kew's first official director Sir William Hooker. Cunningham discovered many hundreds of new plant species including trees, shrubs, palms and ferns, as well as carnivorous plants, and is remembered through the plants named after him. These include the Moreton Bay or hoop pine *Araucaria cunninghamii* (see p. 116), *Banksia cunninghamii,* the myrtle beech *Nothofagus cunninghamii,* and the genera *Cunninghamia* as well as *Alania* of which there is only one species, named – of course – *cunninghamii.*

His writings about the Australian landscape, its wild plants and the people he met are now invaluable historical

An original Cunningham herbarium specimen of the Moreton Bay pine is still available for research in Kew's Herbarium. Cunningham first collected this species at Cape Cleveland on the voyage of the *Mermaid.*

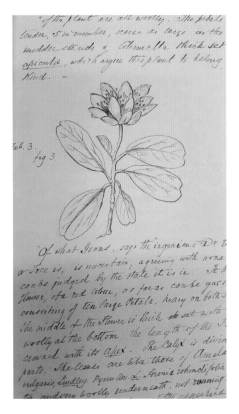

records, as are all of his collections. Kew's archives hold a beautiful notebook of Cunningham's from 1834–1835, when he was at Kew compiling his notes and herbarium specimens for publication. The notebook includes descriptions and drawings of the flora around Shark Bay at the westernmost point of Australia (now a World Heritage Site), including a history of the botanical exploration of the area. The notes are beautiful and detailed, conveying his experienced botanist's eye, with neat descriptive observations on flowers, leaves, stems, seeds and fruits.

For a short time, this industrious, courageous and intelligent botanist was also superintendent of the Royal Botanic Gardens at Sydney. On his death in 1839, aged just 47, his personal herbarium collection was thought to exceed 20,000 specimens, and Kew now holds around 2,000 specimens of his discoveries. His extraordinary achievements in revealing Australia's flora to the world make him one of Kew's most successful collectors and a major contributor to its botanical expertise.

In this intriguing notebook, held in Kew's archives, Cunningham made notes and drawings about the flora of Shark Bay in Western Australia. When in Britain he lived at Strand on the Green, near Kew Bridge, and spent his time arranging his collections and preparing notes for publication.

→ This original drawing, complete with hand-written notes, from Kew's collections shows an orchid (*Thelymitra forsteri*) sent to Kew by Cunningham from New South Wales in 1822.

Received in 1822 from New South Wales from Mr Cunningh

? Bond   Thelymitra forsteri?   June 1823

The name written here "Thelymitra Forsteri?" should refer to a New Zealand
plant. The date pencilled "June 1823" should indicate the date when
the drawing was made - presumably from a plant at Kew.
Allan Cunningham in Hook, Comp. Bot. Mag. II, P. 376, enumerates
Thelymitra Forsteri, Sw. as N. Zealand, Northern Island, Shores of the
Bay of Islands in open fern - lands. - 1826, A. Cunningham.
"Perianthii foliola tres exteriores pallido-purpurea, interiores 3
albce." The ink record seems to have been done later, when a
large collection of such drawings was written up, probably in
part from memory, and may not be correct, for the specific
name is correct, and I see no evidence of this form growing
in Australia, though Bentham has confounded it with
T. nuda, R.Br., an Australian species.   (R.A.R.)
= T. longifolia, Forst. (R&R)

With so many thousands of new plants from around the tropical and temperate worlds flooding into Kew, there was an increasing need for these new species to be properly recorded – both for scientific research and for posterity.

When, in 1790, Banks was introduced to a talented young Austrian artist named Franz Andreas Bauer, he knew this was an opportunity he could not let pass. Franz Bauer was one of three artist brothers, sons of the court painter to the Prince of Liechtenstein. Franz and his brother Ferdinand had gone on to work for Nikolaus von Jacquin, director of the Schönbrunn Imperial Gardens in Vienna, where they had sumptuously illustrated books on new plants coming to the gardens, and perfected the craft of precise botanical art. It was Jacquin's son who brought Franz to England, although he never intended to lose his talents to an English aristocrat. However, Banks lost little time in securing Bauer's services, offering him a generous annual salary to illustrate and immortalise the plant collections at Kew with both accuracy and style.

Bauer became Kew's first botanical artist and was given the title 'Botanick Painter to His Majesty'. He settled into a house on Kew Green and became friends with

Although always highly esteemed, Bauer's work is not as widely known as it should be. Some still regard him as the finest of all botanical artists. This portrait hangs in the main reception of the Herbarium, Library, Art and Archives building at Kew, opposite a bust of Joseph Banks, see p. 8. This portrait is by an unknown artist and was part of Sir William Hooker's own collection.

Delineations of Exotick Plants Cultivated in the Royal Garden at Kew, with paintings by Franz Bauer, was conceived by Banks as an annual publication. It was first published in 1796, but ceased publication in 1803 after its third instalment, having only illustrated 30 plants in total, including this unusual cape heath *Erica massonii*.

Bauer painted a number of
Strelitzia illustrations for his
volume *Strelitzia Depicta*,
including Masson's discovery
Strelitzia reginae. They were
more than likely painted from
living specimens growing at
Kew. The original paintings are
held in Kew's illustrations
collection.

many distinguished botanists, including John Lindley (who went on to help found the Royal Horticultural Society). The paintings he produced were elegant, beautiful and precise, and he and his brother set the bar for what botanical painting should be, a standard which still exists today.

Bauer devoted 50 years of his life to Kew, in which time he saw many thousands of plants come into the gardens. He also saw plenty of developments in horticultural techniques. Great advances in glasshouse technology and heating allowed more tropical species – especially orchids – to thrive, enabling him to paint them. He often used microscopes to assess and understand plant anatomy, becoming adept at dissection. He is described as being probably the first botanical illustrator to create detailed anatomical drawings of plants, vital to their identification.

Banks has been described as 'the first great English promoter of botanical illustration'. Ever since his first voyage he had employed artists to record his discoveries and valued their contributions. In hiring Bauer to work for Kew he created one of the most rewarding artistic partnerships botany has ever seen. And, Franz was not the only brother to benefit from Banks's largesse. Ferdinand was hand-picked by Banks to travel with Captain Matthew Flinders to circumnavigate Australia and record its

This original painting of the early purple orchid (*Orchis mascula*) shows how Bauer portrayed all elements of a plant to aid identification.

natural wonders with botanist Robert Brown and Kew gardener Peter Good. He soon earned a reputation as one of the world's best natural history artists.

Franz Bauer's techniques, talent and professionalism had a clear and lasting influence on Kew and its subsequent botanical artists, ensuring that Kew became home to a stunning collection of botanical art. To this day, Kew continues to support many botanical artists.

Bligh and the breadfruit

Inside one of the old handwritten records books in Kew's archives, where every plant coming in and out of the gardens was recorded, there is an entry entitled 'the year 1793' for a shipment arriving on HMS *Providence* captained by one William Bligh. The consignment of 'Otaheita Plants' (from Tahiti), included four specimens of breadfruit (*Artocarpus altilis*), one of the most important food plants of the Pacific, as well as coconuts, yams and banana plants. The four breadfruit plants were the remainder of a large consignment (of almost 700 plants) that Bligh had just delivered to the West Indies.

A letter (dated 7 February 1793) from Alexander Anderson, superintendent of the well-regarded St Vincent Botanical Garden in the Caribbean to his friend and fellow Scottish botanist William Forsyth, records the arrival of Captain Bligh with his breadfruit cargo on the *Providence*. 'You no doubt before this have heard of the arrival of the Breadfruit Ship, Capn. Bligh . . . is a man of great ability . . . There are about 300 Breadfruit plants . . . with other . . . fruits and useful plants.' Anderson writes that he then put over 400 different new plants on board with Bligh for Kew, and these are also all recorded in flowing

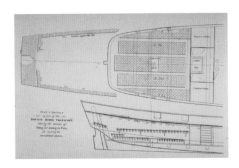

Careful planning was needed to figure out how to fit as many breadfruit plants into the Great Cabin of the *Bounty* as possible.

This letter in Kew's archives relates how Captain Bligh finally delivered breadfruit plants to the St Vincent Botanical Garden.

Artocarpus Incisa, Monocia Monandria.
Incisa — Breadfruit

Drawn by Mrs Hutton
Painted by Mrs M. Hutton II. 1894

handwriting in the 'Inwards' book as being received at the gardens. This was, of course, not the first time Bligh had been on a ship with breadfruit – but it was the first time he had successfully completed a voyage with some.

The breadfruit tree is thought to be native to northern New Guinea but has long been moved around and cultivated across the Pacific islands and South-East Asia. This tall, large-leaved tropical tree produces an abundance of green,

Banks first came across the useful large fruits of the tropical breadfruit tree in Tahiti. This beautiful painting by Janet Hutton (1894) is held in Kew's collection.

spherical, spiny fruits throughout the year. These are full of starch and vitamin C and can be eaten boiled, baked or fried, with a similar taste to potatoes or bread. The tree is also put to many other uses wherever it is grown.

Banks had come across the breadfruit in Tahiti, so was familiar with its usefulness (see p. 22). In 1787, in a typical example of the imperialist thinking of the time, the British Admiralty, Royal Society and Banks decided that breadfruit would be just the thing to help feed the enslaved peoples working on British plantations in the West Indies. The mission to collect and transport it was given to one Lieutenant Bligh and an inexperienced crew on the armed transport ship HMS *Bounty*. On board, to oversee the collection and propagation of the plants, was a Kew gardener-botanist named David Nelson and his assistant, William Brown.

Under Banks's supervision, the captain's cabin was converted to carry over a thousand plants across the ocean to their new homes. The voyage went well initially, with breadfruit plants being propagated successfully during a long stay in Tahiti. Having stowed these aboard, 'in a most flourishing condition', Bligh 'sailed with 1015 Bread Fruit Plants and many Fruit Kind, in all. 774 Pots, 39 Tubs, & 24 Boxes', and the ship headed off on the second part of its mission to the West Indies. The rest of the story is now written into legend,

Bligh was honoured by a genus of plants being named after him – *Blighia*. This painting of it entitled 'Foliage and Fruit of the Akee, Jamaica' by Marianne North is number 137 of 848 in her gallery at Kew.

with a mutiny led by Fletcher Christian on 28 April 1789 ending with Bligh and 18 of his crew put overboard in a small boat and left to sail thousands of miles to Timor. Nelson stayed loyal to Bligh, but Brown remained with the mutineers. Bligh's epic voyage in that tiny vessel was miraculous, but sadly Nelson did not survive the deprivation and died once they reached Timor.

From Jakarta, Bligh wrote an account of the mutiny to Banks, dated 13 October 1790:

> *I am now to relate one of the most atrocious and consummate Acts of Piracy ever committed . . . It may be asked what could be the cause for such a Revolution. In Answer to which I have only to give a description of Otaheite, which has every allurement both to luxury and ease, and is the Paradise of the World.*

Today, this tale has often been romanticised, but the true purpose of the *Bounty* and *Providence* and the implications of their botanical cargo should not be forgotten. In a final twist, having gone to great lengths to move this plant across oceans, its perceived potential as a food crop was never realised.

The St Vincent Botanical Garden in Kingstown, St Vincent and the Grenadines, is believed to be the oldest tropical botanic garden in the world. It has been hugely important in the global movement of plants, and in growing and conserving rare plants, since 1765. This photograph, held in Kew's archives, shows the gardens in the late 19th century.

Plants on the move

George III and Banks often discussed enhancements to the gardens at Kew, and improvements to agriculture in Britain and its colonies, as two sides of the same coin. For the King, keeping his people fed and happy was a primary concern in maintaining a peaceful reign, and significantly added to the success of the British Empire. Plant products were one of the most traded commodities of the day – from sugar and tea to timbers and tobacco – and were a sign of the country's wealth and vitality. It has been estimated that in the 19th century 90 per cent of trade in raw materials was in plants.

Banks wanted Britain to have a good share of this trade, and that meant controlling where the plants grew. If they didn't grow in British-controlled lands then he intended to help try to move them there. During his time supervising Kew, Banks transformed it into a centre of global plant transfer. With the concentration on practical horticulture, the collecting of economic plants, as well as the use of his own vast herbarium and library, Kew's resources became second to none. Plants were brought in, grown, studied, propagated and then shipped out to wherever they might be of most use.

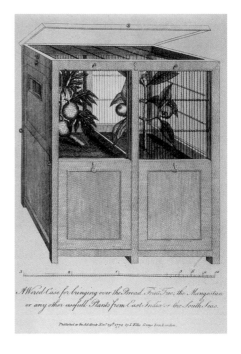

A Wired Case for bringing over the Bread Fruit Tree, the Mangostan or any other usefull Plants from East India or the South Seas.

Published as the Act directs Nov.r 25.th 1774 by I. Ellis Gray's Inn London.

This 18th-century plant case was designed 'for bringing over the breadfruit tree or mangosteen or any other useful plants from the East Indies or the South Seas'. It had room for the plants to be planted in soil and a hinged lid to allow more light and air to reach the plants inside.

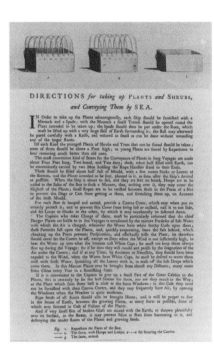

This leaflet from around 1770 by John Fothergill, held in Kew's archives, was given to all his plant collectors to ensure the correct assembling of his plant box and the safe passage of any new plants on board ship.

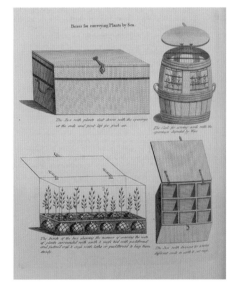

A variety of different types of containers were trialled for effective plant transport in the late 18th century, but the failure rate continued to be high until the invention of the 'Wardian case' in 1829 by Nathaniel Ward. This illustration is from John Lettsom's book *The natural history of the tea-tree* 1799, held in Kew's library.

Moving plants around the globe was a fraught enterprise. Trying to transport live plants on long sea voyages without them succumbing to salt water or wind damage, not to mention neglect, proved extremely challenging. For there to be success at Kew, however, Banks wanted new live plants brought in. He created guidelines for his collectors on packing plants, recommending the 'abundant use of damp moss in casks cut down to manageable sizes with drain holes in the bottom', and telling Cunningham to 'try different methods until you are fully satisfied of the better means of sending home your precious treasures'. There were precise instructions for watering with rainwater, ventilation, and protection from rats, cockroaches and any other animals on board. For dedicated missions, such as that on the *Bounty*, the whole of the Great Cabin was converted with a lead-lined floor and two large skylights to help it act as a sea-going greenhouse (see p. 70). Banks took it upon himself to design various 'plant cabins' or 'botanic conservatories' for ships, to allow specimens to be planted in soil and receive fresh air and water, and these became widely used. He also had to be efficient and mindful when ships docked in order to get the King's plants off the ship as soon as possible.

When Banks sent collectors out around the world they were always told to look for plants with practical uses, as well as beautiful rarities for Kew. Some subterfuge often went on in this regard, with men sent out ostensibly to look for one thing when Banks had given them secret instructions to also collect something more valuable. In *The History of the Royal Botanic Gardens, Kew*, Ray Desmond says that Banks saw no moral wrongdoing in this and that 'the movement of crops from one part of the globe to another and between colonies would enrich the world's larder of food and reduce famine.' His influence with the King, government, Admiralty and others such as the East India Company was to have profound impacts on landscapes and economies across the world.

Plant products – from sugar and tea to timbers and tobacco – were one of the most traded commodities of the day and a sign of the country's wealth and vitality. 'Harvesting the Sugar-Cane in Minas Geraes, Brazil' by Marianne North, 1872.

A taste for tea

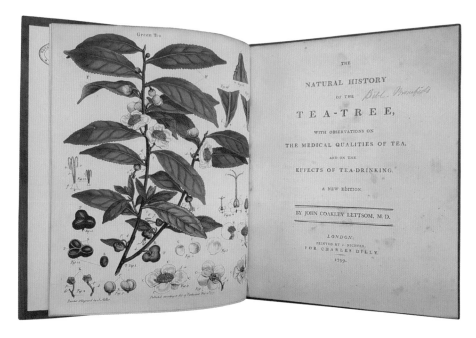

One of the lesser known influences of Joseph Banks, which now has an impact on all of our lives, is the groundwork he laid for the tea industry in Assam. Britain as an empire was always determined to grow its own crops of desirable and useful products rather than having to pay other countries for them, and to their annoyance China still held the trade monopoly on tea. By the mid-1790s Britain was drinking over 23 million pounds of tea a year (21 shiploads), so the commercial potential for new British-owned plantations was immense.

In the 1799 publication *The Natural History of the Tea-Tree*, John Lettsom tried to compile everything that was then known about tea: theories on how it was grown, gathered and dried and how it was drunk in China and Japan, as well as its possible medicinal benefits (with a warning against over-consumption). Banks edited this book for Lettsom. This original edition is from Kew's archives.

Banks envisaged a network of colonial gardens all helping in an endeavour of 'economic botany' – moving plants of use to British trade around the world. He supported the creation of a botanical garden in Calcutta, India, where the climate would support a range of tropical edible plants. Using his considerable network and influence, he organised for tea (*Camellia sinensis*) to be grown at Calcutta for study. He knew it was possible to transport tea plants from previous experiments in Corsica, and in the late 1780s formulated plans to move Chinese tea plants to British-controlled parts of north-east India, where he had deduced the climate and growing conditions would be perfect. He also recommended they were accompanied by expert Chinese tea growers and British commercial gardeners.

However, Chinese tea plants often did not flourish in India and Banks lost his enthusiasm for the project. It was only in 1823 (after Banks's death) when botanist Robert Bruce 'discovered' native Indian tea plants (*Camellia sinensis* var. *assamica*) growing wild in Assam that the possibilities for a profitable tea industry began to really blossom. He sent plants to his brother Charles at the Calcutta Botanic Garden, who successfully grew a great number of them.

The Assam region became hugely significant for tea growing. The first 12 chests of Assam tea were shipped to London in 1838, and by 1890 it was

This late-19th-century photograph from Kew's archives shows how many women were employed to handpick tea leaves in India.

supplying 90 per cent of Britain's tea. Sadly, as history records, India paid an enormous price for this – politically, economically, in lives lost, and on their natural environment as large areas of forest were cleared for plantations. Today, India remains one of the world's largest producers of tea, employing millions of people.

4510.

Mangifera indica, L.

WA-Stebbing .060

Mango.
Mangifera indica
Nov. 12. 1900. *Anacardiaceæ*

Meeting the mango

When Banks sailed on the *Endeavour* with Cook in 1768, one of his first stops was at the beautiful island of Madeira, off the coast of Morocco. He recorded his five-day stay there in great detail in his journal, collecting around 230 species and noting all the fruits and crops grown there including bananas, guava, pineapples and mango. The latter he described as 'about the size of a peach, full of a melting yellow pulp not unlike that of a summer peach which has a very gratefull flavour'.

The favourable view of the mango as well as other tropical fruits was one of the key stimuli in the development of hothouses in Britain. Banks knew that if the technology could be perfected then it would not take long for the tables of the rich to be burgeoning with these delicious fruits, and 'some of them perhaps in less than half a century, be offered for sale on every market day at Covent Garden'. He was always keen to turn plants 'of curiosity' into ones of economic benefit, and the mango was ripe for experimentation. He also saw the opportunities for plants such as the mango to be transferred to more tropical parts of the Empire as nutritious food sources.

Mangoes are native to the Indian subcontinent and have been cultivated for thousands of years. The mango was one of the plants Bligh took to Jamaica on HMS *Providence*. The transfer of mango plants to Kew was seen as a prime example of Kew being 'the botanical metropolis of the world'. Ray Desmond notes in *The History of the Royal Botanic Gardens, Kew* that in 1808 a mango finally ripened at Kew in the autumn. This illustration by Mary Anne Stebbing is held in Kew's collections.

Investigating hemp

In the Age of Sail, hemp became one of the most important plants in the world. Hemp (*Cannabis sativa*) was widely used to make sail cloth, rigging and ropes, all vital for the ships that ensured trade, exploration and supply to and from Britain's colonies.

Hemp was, and still is, a wonderfully useful plant. That its fibres are surprisingly strong has long been known, but its potential as an energy source, building material and even as a food is still largely untapped. In the late 18th century, much of Britain's hemp supply for rope came from Russia, while the hemp grown at home was often too fine or soft for rope making and was used for sail cloth instead. Britain could not produce enough hemp itself and a crisis in supply led to experiments in growing it, and seeking alternatives to it, in other countries such as Canada and India. During the French Revolution, in 1797, Banks was appointed to the Privy Council of Trade and placed in charge of sorting out Britain's hemp trade and supplies. He compiled a complete dossier on the growing, yields, manufacture, supply, profits and potential of hemp, and where it might profitably be grown.

This example of woven hemp rope is from Kew's vast Economic Botany Collection of useful plant products.

In Kew's library is a set of documents he compiled at this time, including a letter by him dated 1801, detailing sending a small quantity of hemp seed to Ireland for experiment, but apologising that he couldn't get hold of more, as so many farmers were now planting it. He describes the similarity of hemp to flax in its growing and processing, and says that profits from an acre of hemp were now at £12 an acre – considerably more than wheat or potatoes. Interestingly, he also mentions that he had recently sent out six local men experienced in hemp production to India, to aid their industry.

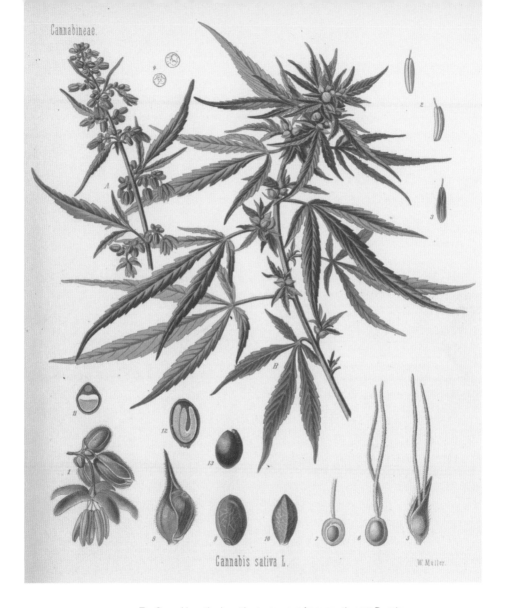

Cannabineae.

Cannabis sativa L.

W. Müller.

Cannabis sativa is native to an area from south-east Russia, across Iran, Afghanistan and Pakistan to north-west China. This coloured illustration of hemp from Kew's library by Walter Müller was completed for Köhler's *Medizinal-Pflanzen*, 1887.

The mysteries of the East

China's plant diversity is unparalleled in the temperate regions of the world, with over 30,000 species – an extraordinary percentage of which are found nowhere else. The south-west is now particularly well known for its botanical riches – the Victorian plant hunter Ernest Wilson referred to China as the 'mother of gardens' because of the number of beautiful garden-worthy plants it offers.

China was effectively closed to the rest of the world during Banks's day, but this did not deter British nurseries and collectors from trying to get hold of its fascinating plants. Banks was utterly delighted to receive the stunning Asian tree peony (*Paeonia suffruticosa*) from one John Duncan in Canton (now Guangzhou) in 1787, for example. To ensure that Kew had the best of what was available, Banks sent William Kerr – another of Kew's promising young Scottish gardeners – to China in 1804. Kerr spent eight years trawling the nurseries and gardens of Canton in southern China, as well as obtaining plants from Macao and Manila. Foreign collectors were often assigned to eminent merchant families in Hong Kong, such as the Pan family, who were adept at seeking out and trading in plants. Kerr became the first Western professional plant collector in China.

The elegant yellow *Rosa banksiae* is now a firm garden favourite. Kerr originally sent back a white form from China. This engraving was produced by Pierre Joseph Redouté for *Choix des Plus Belles Fleurs*, held in Kew's library.

Magnolia purpurea (now *liliiflora*) is native to
south-west China but has been grown for
centuries in China as an ornamental tree. It is
one of the parents of the much more familiar
M. × soulangeana. This painting is from Kew's
Kerr collection (see p. 88).

In all he sent back 238 new species, most of which were completely unknown in Europe, including one that is still very familiar in UK gardens today – the yellow-flowered *Kerria*, which is named after him.

Other well-known plants Kerr sent to Kew included white *Rosa banksiae* 'Alba Plena', which was named after Banks's wife; that now ubiquitous small hedging shrub *Euonymus japonicus*; the tiger lily *Lilium lancifolium*; the pretty flowering shrub *Pieris japonica*, and the hardy *Begonia grandis*.

Following his success in China, Kerr went on to become the superintendent at the King's House gardens in Colombo, Sri Lanka (then Ceylon) in 1812, and joined the list of successful Scottish Kew-trained gardeners that went on to run botanical gardens around the world.

Banks was delighted to receive a Chinese peony from Canton, at a time when few plants were allowed out of China. This stunning illustration is one of a set of paintings by Chinese artists sent to Banks by William Kerr in 1805, now in Kew's collections (see p. 88).

A Chinese collection

While in China, William Kerr commissioned a vast series of drawings and paintings by Chinese artists. These were sent to Kew to illustrate to Banks and Aiton what the plants he was sending to them should look like in their maturity. Kerr would have seen many of these plants growing in the nurseries and traditional gardens around Canton.

This unique collection of over 300 exquisite pieces of art is held in Kew's collections. It is thought to have been commissioned in two sets – both on behalf of Banks. They arrived in London in 1805 and 1807. Unfortunately, no information on the Chinese artists is currently known.

Hibiscus: Probably *Hibiscus rosa-sinensis*, a beautiful evergreen shrub named by Carl Linnaeus in 1753; 'rosa sinensis' translates as rose of China. The five-petaled flowers vary widely in colour.

Bombax: Possibly *Bombax ceiba*, a popular ornamental tropical tree in southern China, also known as the cotton tree due to the white fibres inside its fruit capsules.

Bauhinia corymbosa: Now named *Cheniella corymbosa*, this climbing perennial shrub, with its distinctive lobed leaves, is native to China. It is part of the legume (pea or bean) family as can be seen by its distinctive seedpods.

Nelumbo: The stunning sacred lotus flower (*Nelumbo nucifera*) is more usually associated with India, but it also grows throughout South-East Asia. They are often confused with true waterlilies but this is one of just two species in its own distinct family.

Banks's influence on horticulture

Joseph Banks was by no means the first person in England to set up a botanic garden or to seek to gather rare and unusual plants for study or use by others. He built upon the experience and knowledge of other plantsmen and wealthy English landowners from previous centuries who had amassed prized plant collections – from exotic trees to dazzling tulips. He also followed in the footsteps of more recent men, such as Peter Collinson and John Fothergill, who had private collections and their own collectors overseas, as well as nurseries such as James Gordon's, Lee & Kennedy, Loddiges and others. Such men were not plant hoarders, they shared and sold plants, and were passionate about promoting botany and the practical benefits of natural history for the country. Collinson is most noted for supplying the gentry including the prodigious tree collector, the 3rd Duke of Argyll, with interesting trees and plants. The Duke's garden in Whitton once held over 350 species of trees – some of which later came to Kew. At Kew, Banks followed in the wake of the knowledgeable 3rd Earl of Bute, who had advised Prince Frederick and Princess Augusta on creating Kew's first botanic garden.

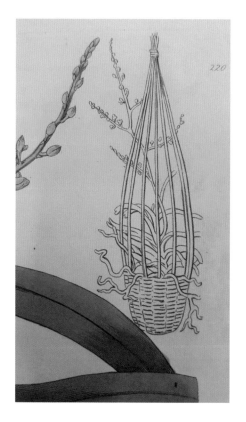

This drawing of an orchid basket was included in *Edwards's Botanical Register* for 1817, which described an orchid known as Sir Joseph Banks's Aerides (*Aerides paniculata*) and reported that Banks had invented a basket for better cultivation of 'epiphytic' orchids.

Kew Gardens, Museum N° 3. — LL.

The 19th century was not just an era of new plant discoveries but also one of huge developments in horticulture: from increasing understanding in growing and breeding a wider selection of plants, to developments in greenhouse technology and cultivation, and in understanding how to control pests and diseases. Eminent garden historian Brent Elliott says, 'in all these fields, Banks played an instigating role, either through his own

Banks knew the limitations of the existing glasshouse technology in buildings such as the Orangery and Great Stove at Kew, and could see great improvements were possible to increase space, light, ventilation and heating. This photograph of the Orangery, from Kew's archives, dates from 1846.

Banks's inventions of plant transport cases (see also p. 74) inspired Nathaniel Ward to invent the 'Wardian case' in 1829. This Kew photo shows a Wardian case being packed in one of Kew's nurseries in the mid-20th century.

activities, or through his patronage and encouragement of others.' Such 'others' included Thomas Knight, who led the way in experimenting with plant propagation and breeding, as well as in other practical considerations such as the correct use of fertilisers and irrigation. Banks's encouragement of Knight meant that he was often seen as Banks's 'protégé'.

Elliott estimates that almost 7,000 plant species were introduced into cultivation in Britain during the reign of George III, 'mainly through the efforts of the collectors that Banks sent out under the auspices of Kew'. The coordination of this effort by Banks, Aiton and their colleagues should not be under-estimated. Banks's work to set Kew on track as a royal botanic garden of worldwide renown was a phenomenal achievement, although his aims in collecting – and not sharing – the King's plants with others were often misunderstood and misrepresented. It remains a great shame, however, that Banks himself did not write and publish more, considering the wealth of knowledge he accumulated over his life. Instead, he used all his influence, through personal and professional networks, to encourage others to do so.

Banks knew the limitations of the greenhouses or 'hothouses' of his day, but as with his experiments with plant cabins on ships' decks, he could also see vast potential for their improvement and development. He encouraged Knight to

Banks brought back specimens of many plants that we now consider extremely garden-worthy, such as hebes, ferns, *Phormium*, and alpines such as this *Celmisia* from New Zealand. This plant was formally described by Sir Joseph Hooker (the second director of Kew) in New Zealand. Hooker was the first to publish a flora of New Zealand, in 1867. This drawing by botanical artist Matilda Smith was completed for *Curtis's Botanical Magazine* in 1882.

write about his experiments with glasshouse design and heating in the *Transactions of the Royal Society* journal. It was not that long after Banks's death in 1820 that the engineering potential for great glasshouses began to be fulfilled, making designs such as the Palm House at Kew possible.

Meanwhile, a horticultural society was thought to be the ultimate way forward in promoting and sharing all the developments happening in horticulture. The idea for such a society came from John Wedgewood and William Forsyth, who then sought Banks's patronage for the scheme. Banks approved, and was initially fundamental in the formation of The Horticultural Society, which first met in 1804 with a handful of members, and in 1805 made Banks its chair. Banks happily engineered the rules and regulations of the Society so that it encouraged all the things he was interested in. This society was, of course, to develop into the mighty Royal Horticultural Society of today, which has continued to promote best practice in horticulture across the country and the world.

Elliott also points out that Banks and his associates laid the foundations for horticulture to become a widely understood and practiced science, and paved the way for the giants of Victorian horticulture who followed, such as Loudon and Lindley, 'to write and share plant knowledge as never before.' From

introducing plants, encouraging plant collectors and breeders, developing rules on seed collecting, encouraging botanical art, promoting technical developments in horticulture and helping set up Kew and the RHS, Banks could not have been more influential on the world of horticulture.

Banks was responsible for bringing many garden-worthy plants back to Britain, including the climber *Bougainvillea spectabilis* - which he collected in Brazil. Marianne North captured its beauty in one of her many paintings at her gallery in Kew.

Banks's lasting impact on Kew

If you walk around Kew Gardens today you can still see some vestiges of Banks's time, although much of the landscape is now of Victorian origin. There are old style glasshouses such as the William Chambers's Orangery, from Princess Augusta's day, as well as follies, which he must have used and visited. There are also plants such as Masson's great cycad *Encephalartos altensteinii*, collected in 1775 in the Eastern Cape province of South Africa, now growing in the Palm House. This was one of the first plants to come to Kew under Banks's direction, and the last one that Banks came to see at Kew before his death (when it produced a cone for the first and only time). It is also possible that some of the many hundreds of North American trees that Banks planted in the early 1770s at Kew may still be alive and well.

Dessiné d'après nature par F.WM Trap

The Eastern Cape great cycad (*Encephalartos altensteinii*), was brought to Kew by Francis Masson (p. 53) and was the last plant Banks came to see at Kew before his death, when it produced a cone. This wonderful illustration of a young specimen of this species is held in Kew's art collections.

Exécuté sur pierre par A.J.Wendel.

A. Arnz & Comp.ᵉ Lith. Editeurs.

CEPHALARTOS ALTENSTEINII, LEHM. MAS.

1977-6267
HLWL 2179

MYRTACEAE

"SNOW GUM"
Eucalyptus
pauciflora
subsp. pauciflora

F

NEW SOUTH WALES

Plant labels are used across Kew (and all other botanic gardens) specifying the correct Latin name of the plant, its country of origin, its collector and a reference accession number. This follows the tradition Banks initiated of allowing all plants to be easily identified for research.

Banks enriched the gardens at Kew and made them into a world-renowned botanic garden and a hub for the global movement and study of plants. He started it on the path to where it is today. But there are more subtle influences too – from how horticulture is now practiced, how plants and seeds are collected from the wild, how herbarium specimens are made, how plants are scientifically described and reliably named, and from the vast library, herbarium and botanical art collection, to the use of simple plant labels, a world-class orchid collection, and the focus on plants of use to wider society.

Kew's horticulture and scientific programmes are now focused on conserving plants for the benefit of all. They also help to provide plant-based solutions for the challenges of our times – just as Banks did in his day, albeit in a very different way. There are now successful global projects saving the wild relatives of crops, medicinal plants and keystone species in endangered habitats. Rather than gathering for King and country and keeping those collections as a royal preserve, Kew is now focused on the ethos of freely sharing its knowledge, resources and historical collections with the world, and it partners with over 120 countries for the benefit of everyone.

Banks was meticulous in how he pressed and preserved plants for future description and research, and the art of creating a good, useful herbarium specimen has been perfected in botanic gardens such as Kew today. This species of orchid (*Oberonia disticha*) from the Society Islands was also collected by Banks.

Banks's plants
Red bottlebrush (*Melaleuca viminalis*)

You can see how these highly ornamental Australian plants got their common name by just looking at their stunning crimson-coloured bottlebrush-like inflorescences. This species (first called *Metrosideros viminalis*) was discovered by Banks and Solander during their stay on the Endeavour River in Queensland in 1770. They found it among the plants of the open forests there, often near flowing water. It usually grows as a large shrub but can reach up to 15 m (50 ft) tall and has weeping branches – earning it another of its common names, the weeping bottlebrush. It is native to temperate regions of Australia's east coast. Its seed capsules can stay on the plant for several years after pollination, and often only open after being subjected to the heat and smoke of wildfires.

Bottlebrushes have become a favourite in gardens and for landscaping and several beautiful cultivars have been developed, including the compact dwarf shrub 'Captain Cook'.

AT KEW: You can see a variety of *Melaleuca* species in the Temperate House and nearby Davies Exploration House.

The Victorian painter Marianne North captured the striking nature of the bottle brush plant in this painting, which is on show in her Kew gallery.

Pōhutukawa (*Metrosideros excelsa*)

Banks collected seven species of *Metrosideros* while in New Zealand on the *Endeavour* voyage. The most familiar of these today is the New Zealand Christmas tree, or pōhutukawa, (*M. excelsa*). This tall evergreen tree puts on a fantastic display of bright red flowers (made up of a mass of stamens) every December. Māori revere this tree for its strength and beauty, and it has great cultural significance. Banks named it *Metrosideros* after its hard heartwood (in Greek *metra* means core and *sideros* means iron). He collected this species in Mercury Bay on the eastern coast of the North Island in November 1769, where Cook observed the transit of Mercury.

Today, 12 species of *Metrosideros* are recognised in New Zealand, and many cultivars exist, but this and other species are now under serious threat from non-native possums (which browse them) and from a fungus called myrtle rust, both of which may severely reduce their numbers.

AT KEW: Head to the Temperate House to discover a delightful specimen of this species.

This original illustration of *Metrosideros tomentosa* by Walter Hood Fitch, dated 1850, is from Kew's vast illustration collection. Fitch was one of the most prolific botanical illustrators at Kew, producing over 12,000 published illustrations, 2,700 of which were for *Curtis's Botanical Magazine*. He was principal artist for the magazine for over 40 years.

Hydrangea macrophylla
'Sir Joseph Banks'

Also known as the big leaf hydrangea, this now familiar garden favourite was first collected in Japan by Carl Thunberg in 1777, who named it *Viburnum macrophyllum* in his 1784 book *Flora Japonica*. It is believed it first arrived in Britain after being smuggled out of China and sent to Joseph Banks in 1788, who then gifted it to Kew. Its huge spherical flowerheads and its propensity to change colour from rose-pink to steely blue depending on the pH of the soil it grows in, gained it a fanbase with Georgian and Victorian gardeners. In the late 18th century it was described and named as *Hydrangea hortensia* but then later became known as *H. macrophylla* 'Joseph Banks'.

AT KEW: You can enjoy a variety of hydrangeas at Kew including those at the Woodland Glade along Cedar Vista.

This engraving of a hydrangea is by Pierre Joseph Redouté (engraved by Langlois). From a copy of *Choix des plus belles fleurs: prises dans différentes familles du règne végétal, et de quelques branches des plus beaux fruits* held at Kew.

Hortensia.

Gum trees (*Eucalyptus*)

Banks collected the first specimen of *Eucalyptus* while at Thirsty Sound in Queensland, Australia (halfway between Brisbane and Cairns), which Sydney Parkinson dutifully drew. However, it was not named until much later as *E. crebra* or the red ironbark – one of the most common and toughest trees of the eastern coast forests.

The genus name *Eucalyptus* was not coined until 1788, when Kew's David Nelson brought back a specimen from a stop at Tasmania on Cook's third voyage. That specimen was examined by a French botanist at Kew called Charles Louis L'Héritier de Brutelle and named *Eucalyptus obliqua* – or the messmate stringybark.

Eucalypts are a diverse group of trees with over 700 species now known. They are keystone species in the ecology of Australian forests, their leaves are vital food for koalas and their flowers are a source of nectar for many other species.

Today, they are also planted around the world as garden and landscaping trees, although you would be wise to avoid planting *E. regnans* – which is the world's tallest broadleaved tree, growing up to 114 m (374 ft).

This illustration of *Eucalyptus stricta* (or the Blue Mountains mallee ash) was drawn by Kew artist Matilda Smith in 1889. This species is native to eastern New South Wales where Banks explored (although he did not collect it), and it is thought that Cook was the first person to coin the common name of 'gum tree' for all eucalypts.

Peter H. Raven Library/Missouri Botanical Garden

Saw banksia (*Banksia serrata*)

Banks collected a total of four different banksias while in Australia, the first of which was the saw banksia (*B. serrata*) at Botany Bay in April/May 1770. Solander originally named it *Leucadendrum serratifolium*, but it was re-named *Banksia serrata* in Banks's honour by Carl Linnaeus's son in 1782. This genus of plants was chosen above all others brought back on the *Endeavour* voyage to honour Banks and his contributions to botany.

The saw banksia is still a common species in eastern Australia. This and other banksias are characteristic of open, dry forests and are an integral part of their ecology. Their unique flowers offer valuable nectar to a variety of insects, birds, invertebrates and mammals.

Banksias now number around 170 species, with all but one being endemic to Australia. The species in this unusual genus range in size from small shrubs to trees 30 m (98 ft) tall.

AT KEW: You can find a variety of *Banksia* species in the Temperate House and Davies Exploration House.

The saw banksia produces magnificent inflorescences as seen in this illustration in *Edwards's Botanical Register* of 1830. See also p.123.

Small-leaved kōwhai (*Sophora microphylla*)

While in New Zealand in late 1769, Banks came across the evergreen trees known locally at kōwhai in several places. He took seeds back to Britain, arriving in 1771. This relatively common species of kōwhai (*Sophora microphylla*) is now New Zealand's unofficial national flower. It has unusual elongated yellow flowers, which hang from the stems like golden bells among its glossy small pinnate leaves. It is a popular garden tree in New Zealand, growing 4–8 m (13–26 ft) tall. Several parts of this plants are poisonous, especially its ripe seeds.

Today, one of the best-known cultivars of this tree is called 'Sun King'. It adds stunning colour to a British garden in late winter and early spring.

AT KEW: Discover specimens of this species in the Temperate House and several growing outside at Kew's wild botanic garden, Wakehurst, in West Sussex.

This W. H. Fitch painting from 1840 for *Curtis's Botanical Magazine* perfectly captures this beautiful New Zealand plant.

The Moreton Bay or hoop pine
(*Araucaria cunninghamii*)

The Moreton Bay pine, or hoop pine, was discovered by Banks's Australian plant collector Allan Cunningham (see p. 60) on the shores of Moreton Bay near Brisbane, in 1824. Banks himself had seen this tree in 1770; it had also been seen by Banks's botanist Robert Brown, on Captain Flinders' voyage in 1774. According to Cunningham, both previous examinations had concluded it was the same as the Norfolk Island pine (*Araucaria heterophylla*). However, Cunningham thought differently and collected it to bring back to Kew, whereupon it was properly examined and given its own species name.

An ancient conifer species, the hoop pine is native to the dry forests of north New South Wales and eastern Queensland. Hoop pines grow very slowly but become beautiful tall majestic trees when mature. One of the largest remaining forests of hoop pine can be found in Lamington National Park on the border of New South Wales and Queensland.

This illustration of the hoop pine is from Kew's copy of the limited edition 1839 volume entitled *Pinetum woburnense* - which illustrated all the special conifers collected by the then Duke of Bedford at Woburn Abbey.

Passiflora aurantia

Blunt-leaved passionfruit (*Passiflora aurantia*)

Banks collected two species of passionflower on the *Endeavour* voyage – *Passiflora aurantia* in Australia and *P. tetrandra* in New Zealand. *Passiflora aurantia*, the blunt-leaved passionfruit, is one of three native Australian passionflowers. Banks spotted this unusual climbing species for the first time at the Bay of Inlets in Queensland, in 1770. It its homeland, it blooms generously over winter and spring, with each flower first appearing cream or pale pink before maturing to an orange-red. The flowers are followed by small purple ovoid fruits which are not particularly edible.

This stunning species has become prized as a garden plant in both semi-tropical and temperate gardens (although it is not hardy). The engraving created from Sydney Parkinson's original drawing features alongside Banks on a 2018 official Royal Mail 2nd class stamp, created to mark the 250th anniversary of Cook setting sail on the *Endeavour*.

AT KEW: You can enjoy a variety of stunning *Passiflora* species in the Princess of Wales Conservatory.

This species appears in *The Botanist's Repository of new and rare plants* by Henry Andrews, where it is called the Norfolk Island passionflower. It was described as being introduced to Britain in 1792 as seed, from which it was first grown at a Hammersmith nursery. Andrews' ten volume set published between 1797 and 1811 can be found in Kew's library.

Pelargoniums

A plant that we now take for granted as a windowsill staple was once a flower of great rarity and desire. Kew's first plant hunter, Francis Masson (see p. 53), sent 47 species of *Pelargonium* to the gardens from South Africa. These were grown on in Kew's hothouses and trialled outdoors to test their hardiness. They quickly became very popular in nurseries and their place on our windowsills and in our gardens became assured.

Some of Masson's introductions are particularly still enjoyed today – especially the scented-leaf species such as the oak-leaf geranium *Pelargonium quercifolium* and pine geranium *P. denticulatum*.

By 1789, Aiton had listed 102 species of *Pelargonium* in *Hortus Kewensis*. Today, we know that there are around 280 species, over 200 of which are native to South Africa.

AT KEW: Seek out the many pelargonium species and varieties in the Princess of Wales Conservatory.

This image of *Pelargonium denticulatum* is from a stunning set of illustrated volumes by Robert Sweet (1820-30) on the 'Geraniaceae' held in Kew's library.

Fuchsias

Banks was passionate about all of his plant introductions to Kew and often wanted to inspect them as soon as they arrived at the gardens. It is said that when the scarlet fuchsia (*Fuchsia coccinea*) arrived from South America he carried it carefully into the greenhouse on his head 'not choosing to trust it to any other person'. The following year (presumably when it flowered) it was hailed as 'a plant of peculiar beauty' in the gardening press. Specimens were said to cost one guinea each in 1789 – equivalent to over £100 today.

Fuchsias are named after Leonhart Fuchs (1501–1566), a German botanist and author of a notable 16th century herbal. Although the first fuchsia was discovered in the late 17th century by Charles Plumier, they do not seem to have reached Britain until *F. coccinea* arrived from Brazil in 1788 with one Captain Firth, who then gave it to Kew. As more species began to arrive from South America, a craze for fuchsias soon began.

AT KEW: Head to the Temperate House and Agius Evolution Garden to see a range of hardy and half-hardy fuchsias on display.

This engraving of a scarlet fuchsia by Pierre Joseph Redouté is from *Choix des plus belles fleurs: prises dans différentes familles du règne végétal, et de quelques branches des plus beaux fruits* in Kew's library.

A global legacy

Banks lived through an extraordinary and exciting time, one of seemingly endless discoveries and the expansion of the known world – an 'Age of Wonder'. His life, despite the contradictions and controversies that we may see today, was one of extraordinary achievement, and he clearly proved that there was more to him than his privileged upbringing. His utter fascination with the beauty, uniqueness and usefulness of plants – from breadfruit to hemp – was intrinsic to his being. The range of activity he undertook, and the number of plants he was responsible for describing, collecting and bringing to Britain, was unparalleled.

While historians and indigenous communities have plenty to discuss as to his global legacy, the science of botany undoubtedly owes his fierce intellect and enthusiasm a great debt. Without his endless pursuit of knowledge and his support for the natural sciences, horticulture and botanical art, Kew, and many other collection-based institutions around the world, would be very different places.

From hosting 'networking' botanical breakfasts, supporting the careers of naturalists, collectors and artists, being president of the Royal Society for an

By the end of his life Banks had become a baronet and a Knight Commander of the Order of the Bath (its ribbon and star are being worn here), and had achieved great influence over many of Britain's scientific and horticultural institutions. He died on 19 June 1820. The original painting of this engraving is from the Royal Society's collection.

Wellcome Collection

astonishing 41 years, to the global reach of his endless letter writing, Banks was a man of immense influence. He inspired other revolutionary scientists such as Alexander von Humboldt, and in turn Charles Darwin. It was due to Banks's sway with the Admiralty that naturalists (and artists) were taken on board long sea voyages as a matter of course, paving the way for future scientific discoveries – and for Darwin to head off on HMS *Beagle*.

Without Banks's vision, Kew may simply have remained a small royal garden in a London suburb. The select set of Banks's artefacts, letters, herbarium specimens and plants that remain at the gardens, as well as many others belonging to the people he supported and influenced, are precious and tangible links to how he shaped Kew into a place of both botanical pilgrimage and global importance.

There remains an enduring fascination with the *Endeavour* voyage, and its discoveries, collections and legacy continue to be discussed today, especially as cultural objects begin to be repatriated, and native plant conservation projects are needed in the countries the crew visited. Banks's part in that expedition is one of the main reasons that it remains famous to this day. I hope you'll agree that his life story is truly one long botanical adventure.

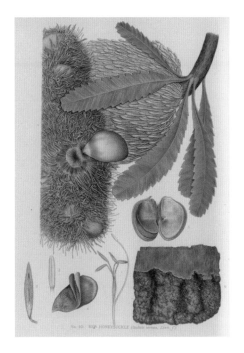

Banksia serrata is a widespread species in the dry forests along the eastern coast of Australia, so it is no surprise that Banks collected it. The pale yellow or cream-coloured upright inflorescences are around 12 cm tall (almost 5 inches). The large stiff leaves are noticeably serrated – leading to its species name 'serrata' and common name of saw banksia. Its other popular common name is 'old man banksia' due to its generally gnarled appearance. This illustration is from *Edwards's Botanical Register*, 1830.

Sources and further reading

The Endeavour Journal of Sir Joseph Banks: Read online at http://gutenberg.net.au/ebooks05/0501141h.html

Aughton, P. (1999) *Endeavour: Captain Cook's First Great Voyage*, Windrush Press

Banks, R. E. R., Elliot, B. et al. (1994) *Sir Joseph Banks: A Global Perspective*, Royal Botanic Gardens, Kew

Carter, H. B. (1988) *Sir Joseph Banks*, British Museum

Chambers, N. (2016) *Endeavouring Banks: Exploring Collections from the Endeavour Voyage*, Paul Holberton Publishing

Davidson, J. (2019) *The Cook Voyages Encounters*, Te Papa Press

Desmond, R. (2007) *The History of the Royal Botanic Gardens Kew*, second edition, Royal Botanic Gardens, Kew

Frame, W. & Walker, L. (2018) *James Cook: The Voyages*, British Library Publishing Division

Gascoigne, J. (1994) *Joseph Banks and the English Enlightenment: Useful Knowledge and Polite Culture*, Cambridge University Press

Gooding, M., Mabberley, D. & Studholme, J. (2017) *Joseph Banks' Florilegium: Botanical Treasures from Cook's First Voyage*, Thames and Hudson

Harrison, C., & Kirkham, T. (2019) *Remarkable Trees*, Thames and Hudson

Holmes, R. (2009) *The Age of Wonder: How the Romantic Generation Discovered the Beauty and Terror of Science*, Harper Press

Lack, W. (2015) *The Bauers Joseph, Franz & Ferdinand: An Illustrated Biography*, Prestel

Lysaght, A. M. (1971) *Joseph Banks in Newfoundland & Labrador, 1766*, Faber and Faber

Mabberley, D. (2017) *Painting by Numbers: the life and art of Ferdinand Bauer*, New South Publishing

O'Brian, P. (2016) *Joseph Banks: A Life*, Folio Society

Parkinson, S. (1773) *A Journal of a Voyage to the South Seas in his Majesty's Ship, The Endeavour*

Stearn, W. T. (1969) 'A Royal Society Appointment with Venus in 1769', *Notes and Records of the Royal Society of London*, 24:1, pp. 64-90.

Stearn, W. & Stewart, J. (1993) *The orchid paintings of Francis Bauer*, Timber Press

Wulf, A. (2013) *Chasing Venus: the race to measure the heavens*, Windmill Books

Index

One of Joseph Banks's walking sticks was gifted to Kew in 1851 by the Rev. Professor J. S. Henslow - a keen botanist and friend of William Hooker and Charles Darwin. The stick is thought to be made from sugar cane.

First published in 2020
Royal Botanic Gardens, Kew, Richmond, Surrey, TW9 3AB, UK
www.kew.org
ISBN 978 1 84246 715 2

Distributed on behalf of the Royal Botanic Gardens, Kew in North America by the University of Chicago Press, 1427 East 60th Street, Chicago, IL 60637, USA.

British Library Cataloguing in Publication Data
A catalogue record for this book is available from the British Library

Design and page layout: Nicola Erdpresser
Cover design: Christine Beard
Project manager: Lydia White
Production manager: Jo Pillai
Copy-editing: Michelle Payne
Proofreading: Sharon Whitehead

Front cover images, clockwise from top: *Banksia coccinea*, View of the Bay of Rio and Sugar Loaf Mountain, Sir Joseph Banks, HM Bark *Endeavour*.
Back cover image: 18th-century plant case.
Endpapers: maps of Kew from 1771

Printed and bound in the UK by Gomer Press Limited

For information or to purchase all Kew titles please visit shop.kew.org/kewbooksonline or email publishing@kew.org

Kew's mission is to be the global resource in plant and fungal knowledge and the world's leading botanic garden.

Kew receives approximately one third of its funding from Government through the Department for Environment, Food and Rural Affairs (Defra). All other funding needed to support Kew's vital worscomes from members, foundations, donors and commercial activities, including book sales.